"Change yourself and change the world."
Anonymous

Your Rebel Plans

Rebel Diva Book Two

Build Your Future
28 days to design a treasure map to your life's dreams.

Own Your Life. Be a Rebel Diva.

Copyright ©2019 Tikiri Herath
Edition: 2019
Library & Archives Canada Cataloging in Publication
ISBN: 978-1-989232-04-0

Author: Tikiri Herath
Publisher: The Rebel Diva Academy®
Proofread and Editing: Stephanie Parent
Copy Editing: Deborah Dove
Cover Design: Angela O e-covers
Formatting: Aelurus Publishing
Author Shot: Aura Mckay

All rights reserved. The use of any part of this publication, reproduced, transmitted in any form or by any means electronic, mechanical, photocopying, recording, or otherwise or stored in a retrieval system without prior written consent of the publisher—or in the case of photocopying or other reprographic copying, a license from the Canadian Copyright Licensing Agency—is an infringement of the copyright law.

Tikiri

The advice and strategies contained here may not be suitable or applicable to everyone or to every situation. Reading this work does not construe an engagement between the author/publisher and the reader, and the author/publisher is not rendering any legal, psychological, accounting or any other professional services through this work. Neither the author nor the publisher will be liable for damages arising from here.

The books and website links cited here are only for information and educational purposes and does not mean the author or the publisher endorses everything provided via these external resources. While the author will make every effort to ensure the links in this book remain updated, there is no guarantee the external sites may always be available or provide what they had initially.

TABLE OF CONTENTS

Rebel Defined	vii
Who This Book Is For	viii
An Exclusive Gift	xi
The Fire in Your Belly	13
The Heroine's Journey	21
The Passion Pyramid	25
INTRODUCTION	31
SECTION One: My Goals	89
SECTION Two: My Execution Plan	133
SECTION Three: My Check-ins	175
SECTION Four: My Schedule	217
SECTION Five: My Pledge	239
SECTION Six: Bonus Questions	243
Exclusive Gift	256
About the Author	262
A Free Story	263

Own Your Life. Be a Rebel Diva.

Rebel

NOUN

plural: rebels

Pronunciation /ˈrɛb(ə)l/

A person who resists authority, control, or convention.

Diva

NOUN

plural: divas

Pronunciation /ˈdēvə/

Goddess. Feminine of divus divine. Late 19th century Italian derived from Latin.

I dedicate this book to *you.*

These books are for you if you long, more than anything, to burst out of your shell into the open and live the life you dream about.

To you I say, never stop dreaming. And never, ever give up the pursuit of your passions.

Do you have dreams you yearn to reach? Do you ache to get unstuck from the life you have today?

If you do, this book is for you.

The second Rebel Diva book, Your Rebel Plans, is all about architecting your future.

Take the next few weeks to go through the exercises in this workbook and create a treasure map for your life dreams using practical and time-tested planning tools.

There are no magic pills or silver bullets to get you to your dreams. It will be work, have no doubt about it. But it will be work you'll enjoy doing. And remember, planning is only 5 percent of your trip. Action constitutes the remaining 95 percent.

What you'll need from here on is a spirit for adventure. You must be open to possibilities, not fear the journey, be tenacious in every step and above all, learn to live in the moment and enjoy the views along the way.

And with that, let's go create the treasure map to your dreams!

Your Rebel Plans

The Rebel Diva Workbooks

www.RebelDivas.com

Sign up to get your exclusive gift!

This Rebel Diva booklet comes with three essential decision-making tools to help you overcome any anxieties when faced with life's challenges. Click on the cover or go to the link below to get your free copy and also learn about exclusive and free training at the Rebel Diva Academy.

https://www.rebeldivas.com/rebel-plans-gift/

Bust Your Fears

Your Rebel Plans

> *"I wish I were a girl again, half savage and hardy and free...
> Why am I so changed? I'm sure I should be myself were I once
> among the heather on those hills."*
> *Emily Brontë*

A FIRE IN YOUR BELLY

We all hold a precious dream within us—a fire burning in our belly.

Yes, every one of us.

Some of us hide our dreams because we're too scared to look our truth in the face. Some of us have valiantly tried to bring those dreams out in the open but quickly stashed them away because of what someone said or how someone judged us. Then, there are some of us who ignore our dreams, pretending they don't exist because acknowledging them would mean we'd be compelled to do something.

The result is graveyards full of women who've been buried with their dreams untouched. Imagine what they could have achieved if they'd stood proudly and taken ownership of their future. Imagine what inspiration they'd have given to the next generation of girls, creating a ripple effect that uplifts us all.

THE WORLD IS YOURS

We're all capable, more than capable, of bringing our dreams to light.

Yes, that means you.

This world can be yours. The future can be yours. All you need to do is bravely step up, grab life by the horns and ride it. You must take ownership of your future. No one else can do that for you. And there is no better time to start your life's amazing ride than today.

IGNORE THE NAYSAYERS

Why do we wait for a life-changing event like sickness, death, layoff, bankruptcy, separation, or divorce—times when we don't have a choice but to wake up and make drastic changes? Why let others dictate who we are and what we must do?

Most people go through their days in a trance without understanding who they truly are, what they're doing or where they're going.

We, especially women, feel burdened by the expectations others put on us, or many times, by the demands we place on ourselves. Without a clear vision for our lives, we're easily manipulated to meet the interests of others—people who've already figured out what they want in life.

Naysayers can be persistent and hard to ignore, especially if they're family and friends. But if you can summon the courage to stand in your power, you'll get an enormous boost in your energy, vitality, and happiness. This will catapult you to your dream life.

Remember, how others judge us is only a reflection of their own insecurities, fears, and worries, or their need to keep us under their control.

SUMMON YOUR COURAGE

So, stop listening to what they say and start following your dreams right this minute.

Where do we start?

First, find an ounce of courage inside you.

Then, do some soul-searching and look for those aspirations longing to jump out. Protect and nurture those dreams.

Finally, you must act. All the dreaming and wishing and hoping in the world won't make anything come alive. Only pure action will do so.

This doesn't have to be scary or difficult. This can be a fun and fulfilling ride. And you're not alone. We will take this journey together.

These books were designed to take you by the hand on an expedition of self-discovery, goal setting, and habit-forming so you can start living your life—the one you wish to have, not the one others expect of you.

Don't be afraid to stand at the edge of your comfort zone. Feel that tingle of fear mixed with excitement and give it a whirl with plenty of support and cheering from the rest of us. You'll find your sense of self-worth grow and your inner strength surge. You'll wake up every day feeling good about yourself and confident in who you are.

More importantly, your vision will expand and you'll see beyond yourself. And this is where magic happens. When you grow, the lives of those surrounding you will also grow. You'll become an amazing role model for your daughters, your sisters, your neighbors, your colleagues, and more.

This is what will make you a true Rebel Diva. A strong and proud woman who stands in her own power and inspires those around her. You'll become the wonder woman we all look up to.

Now, isn't that a life worth living?

Your Rebel Plans

"An unexamined life is not worth living."
Socrates

MY GOAL

My aim is to shake you out of your complacency and to spur you to uncover the wonderful gifts you have within you. I want to see you burst out with confidence and a dazzling smile on your face that says, Watch out world, here I come!

BUT THESE BOOKS AREN'T FOR EVERYONE

I could have easily created a few pop quizzes and slapped on a sexy title like "The One-Minute Passion Finder," and sold a ton of books. But I'd be lying.

I could have filled pages and pages with pointless platitudes to make you feel good about staying stuck where you are and make a handsome profit. But I'd be cheating.

These books don't give you false shortcuts or magic bullets to solve your problems. I call things as they are and don't mince my words.

So, if you don't want to hear hard truths or ask introspective questions, these workbooks aren't for you. If you dislike addressing issues head-on or if you're not a fan of political incorrectness, I urge you not to read further. It will only aggravate you and I'd hate to do that to you.

If, however, you're looking for practical tips that give you results and don't mind language that is to the point, then read on.

LASTING CHANGE

Change requires courage. And courage requires conviction. These books are for the women of this world who yearn to empower themselves and seek that courage to follow their own path and live true to their calling.

But that kind of lasting change doesn't happen overnight. You must do the work and stay consistent as you walk toward your dreams.

If you're prepared to go against everything you've been taught and do the things most won't dare, these books will open new horizons for you. If you are willing to do the work to enhance your inner strength and create a new future, you're in the right place.

In these workbooks, you'll find how to feed the fire burning in your belly. You'll get in touch with your passions. And you'll feel the fear but do it anyway, without worrying about what others think or say.

And that, my dear sisters, is what will make you a true Rebel Diva.

"Choices may be unbelievably hard but they're never impossible.

To say you have no choice is to release yourself from responsibility.

And that's not how a person with integrity acts."

Patrick Ness

Your Rebel Plans

*"I am a woman with thoughts and questions and shit to say.
I say if I'm beautiful. I say if I'm strong.
You will not determine my story – I will."
Amy Schumer*

THE HEROINE IS YOU. THE JOURNEY IS YOUR LIFE.

THE HEROINE'S JOURNEY

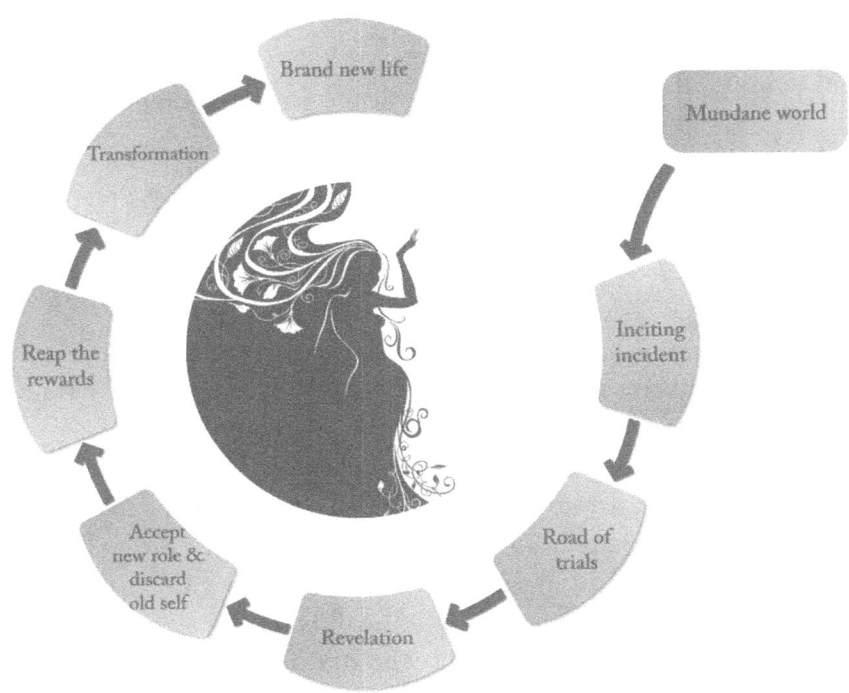

The heroine's journey* is universal. It applies to you whether you are the southern hemisphere or the northern one. It pertains to you regardless of your culture, religion, age, race, sexual orientation or anything else that makes you human.

We all start at stage one—the everyday world—until an incident too arduous for us to handle falls on us, forcing us through this cycle. If we're not ready, the road ahead can be a treacherous one with many troubles along the way.

Some of us may never recover from the inciting incident and succumb to it. Others may get lost, taking wrong turns and feeling every strain of their journey. Then, there will be some of us who will carry on pretending to live in the same ordinary world, though everything has changed. We'll be living an illusion which will cause us to crash and burn even faster than the original event.

We all undergo this cycle in our lives. And for some of us, more than once. It's inevitable. It's what being human is all about.

So, what do we do?

Here are two questions to ask yourself:

- Am I going to sit and wait for life-changing events to trip me up, or can I proactively create the life I deserve starting today?
- Am I going to think of negative incidents as hopeless failures, or can I look at them as calls to adventure—a call to creating a brand-new life?

We're all going to come across times when we feel sorrow, anger, or fear. These emotions may come from something that happened, what someone said, or even a mistake we made that leaves us berating ourselves for days on end. Feeling bad (in its many forms) is normal. It's when we don't face our emotions, run away from them or blame others that problems arise.

We have to learn to acknowledge our feelings. We need to look at what happened dead straight in the eye and decide how we will respond to it. We must take control of how we resolve the difficult things in life. This means pushing our fears and worries away and moving over to the driver's seat to become the navigators of our own futures.

In these pages, you'll find the ideas and concepts that put you in the driver's seat. This doesn't mean you'll be immune to the troubles of life, but you'll get the foresight, the tools, and the knowledge to maneuver your way around them with the least pain and the most gain to you.

Are you ready to become the heroine of your own life?

Based on Joseph Campbell's legendary theory of the twelve-step Hero's Journey.

Your Rebel Plans

THE PASSION PYRAMID

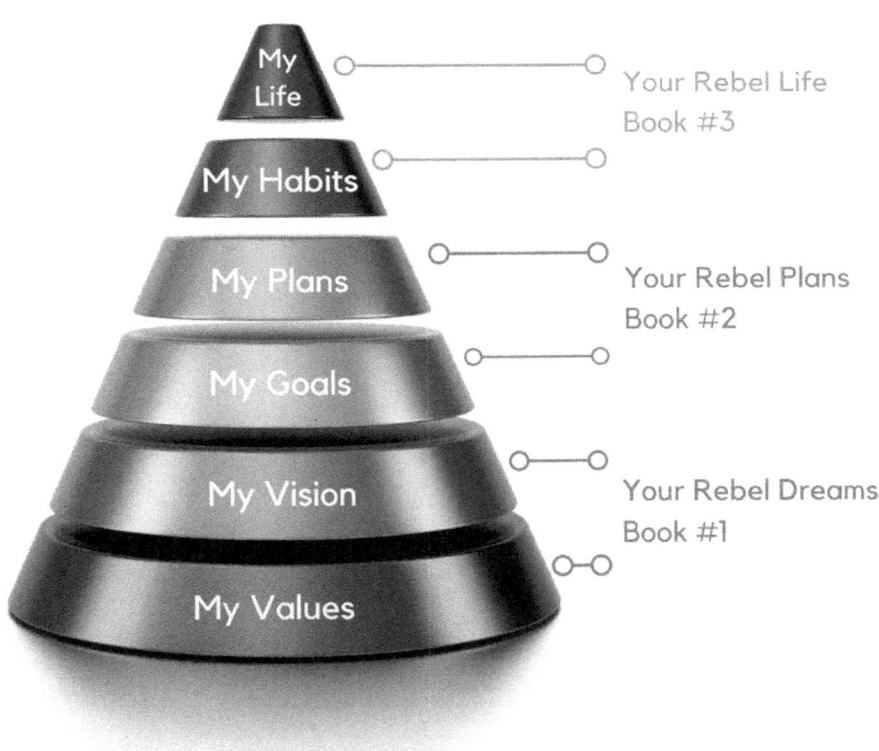

Your Rebel Plans

> *"I am no bird and no net ensnares me. I am a free human being with an independent will."*
> *Jane Eyre*

THE PASSION PYRAMID

You'll need a clear vision and a roadmap to take control over your life. You'll also need to embrace the right mindset and good habits to create the life you desire.

The mandate of this Rebel Diva series is to provide you with that knowledge and skill, with easy-to-follow exercises based on the all-encompassing Passion Pyramid.

As the pyramid shows, your personal values form the base for your life vision, your vision determines your goals, and your goals formulate your plans.

Ultimately, your vision, your goals, and your plans are sustained by your daily habits and mindset.

For this to work, you must:

- Be uncompromising on your personal values
- Be resolute in your life vision
- Be intentional, yet savvy, with your goals
- Be focused on but adaptable with your plans
- Be regular and consistent in your habits

THE REBEL DIVA BOOKS

Each of the Rebel Diva books focuses on a couple steps of this pyramid, moving from the base to the top.

The first book—*Your Rebel Dreams*—helps you uncover your why, that is, your purpose and your passions, culminating in your what, which is your vision.

The second book—*Your Rebel Plans*—shows you how to design a life around your new vision. It captures the stages of goal setting, action planning, and tracking your progress.

The third book—*Your Rebel Life*—helps you create and foster the right habits in the ten most important pillars of your life so you can pursue your aspirations with joy.

Tikiri

THIS BOOK BELONGS TO

Rebel Diva	
Location	
Date	

PRINT EXERCISES IN BOOK

Download the PDF worksheet booklet for *Your Rebel Plans*.

This 100+ page booklet includes worksheets for all the exercises in this book. You can print them, write your answers directly on them, pin them up if you'd like and refer to them every day.

Tap on the link below to download your free private copy.

Your Rebel Plans Worksheet Booklet

https://www.rebeldivas.com/rebel-plans-gift/

INTRODUCTION

LET'S BEGIN THIS JOURNEY!

Your Rebel Plans

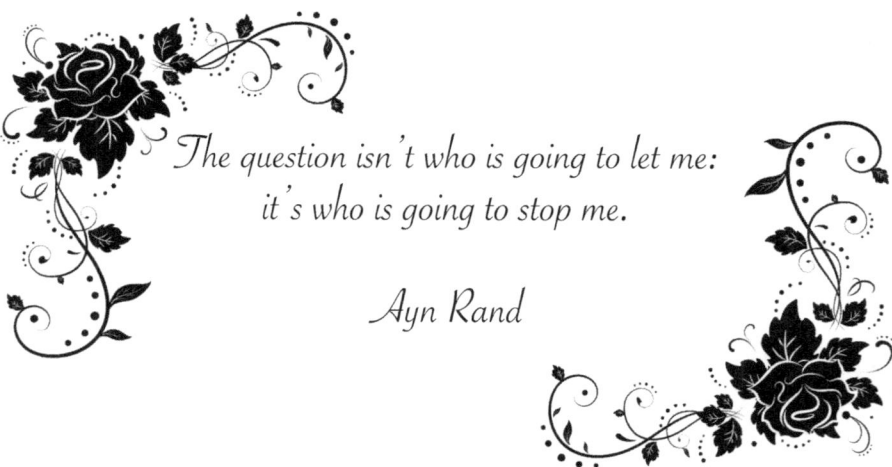

The question isn't who is going to let me: it's who is going to stop me.

Ayn Rand

"Don't let anyone rob you of your imagination, your creativity, or your curiosity. It's your place in the world; it's your life. Go on and do all you can with it, and make it the life you want to live."
Mae C. Jemison

MY BIG AUDACIOUS VISION

Your big audacious vision is the culmination of the self-discovery journey you took in the first workbook: *Your Rebel Dreams*.

Keep in mind though, this vision isn't carved in stone and is certainly not the only vision you'll have in your lifetime. We humans, have longer lifespans than ever before. Many ardent women go on to second, third, or even fourth careers, excelling at each of their exploits. But we've all got to start somewhere.

We must move if we want to get anywhere, and the vision you crafted in the first book is the one we'll explore further here.

If you haven't read the first book in the Rebel Diva series but you have a clear vision for your life, that's great. You don't have to have read *Your Rebel Dreams* to come up with what you want in life but if you are looking for a structured process to identify your purpose in life, uncover your passions and create a life vision, that book will help.

The aim of this second Rebel Diva workbook is to follow a time-tested model to create an execution plan for that vision of yours. This is a fancy way to say we will bring your vision into reality.

We'll break your vision down into practical steps and phases so you'll know what you need to do next. You'll also get the tools to track and measure your progress as you go through this phase of your journey.

From book one, *Your Rebel Dreams*, copy your big audacious vision here. Or write the vision you have created yourself.

Then, every time you start a new section in this book, come back to this page to make sure the work you're planning always aligns with your overarching vision.

MY BIG AUDACIOUS VISION

"Other people will call me a rebel, but I just feel like I'm living my life and doing what I want to do. Sometimes people call that rebellion, especially when you're a woman."
Joan Jett

LIMITATIONS WE PUT ON OURSELVES

Ninety-eight percent of people in the world never even try to achieve their dreams.

According to a study by the Oxford Academic *Social Forces* journal, only 6 percent of adults end up doing what they dream of as children. Behind these numbers are many people who have surrendered their lives and will one day get buried with their unborn dreams still inside.

If you think about it, these people will have died before they're dead. How sad is that?

One of the biggest roadblocks to success in life—whichever way you define success and in whatever area of your life—is how you perceive your life and what you believe in about yourself. Here are the top five reasons most people give for not pursuing their dreams. Do you recognize any of these?

1. I don't have the time.
2. I don't have the money.
3. I'm scared to fail.
4. My friends will judge me.
5. I'm not good enough.

Let's tackle each of these limitations head-on, one by one. Then, on the next page, you'll go through an exercise where you'll look at if and how these limitations impact your own life.

1. I DON'T HAVE THE TIME

When someone says they don't have the time to pursue their goals, they mean "I haven't prioritized my dreams."

How many people waste time on distractions they've created for themselves so they don't have to think about their dreams slipping by?

What if, instead of watching mindless television or getting lost in social media rabbit holes for hours, we practice a new craft? What if we say goodbye to people, places, and persuasions that drown us in drama and instead spend time on things that take us closer to our goals? What if we read a how-to blog, make a plan, take a course or seek a mentor to help us achieve our aspirations?

What would happen if, instead of complaining about not having time, we take one baby step in the direction we want to go?

If you truly desire your dreams, you will make it a priority in your life.

2. I DON'T HAVE THE MONEY

When someone says they don't have enough money, they haven't explored all the options.

You may not need as much capital as you think to achieve your goals. There are countless paths to getting a dream off the ground with little to start. This could include saving up for a few years, taking out a loan, getting part-time work, finding a second job, asking friends or family for support, seeking venture funds, looking for government grants, and starting small and lean, among many other alternatives.

If you really want it, you'll find a way to make it happen. Most entrepreneurs, like myself, bootstrap their ideas and find as many innovative ways as possible to kick-start the project and keep the momentum going. Most times, it's when you search outside conventional thinking patterns or wisdom that you ignite new concepts and ideas.

Many people who have succeeded beyond their wildest imaginations—as business owners or as employees—started off in worse financial situations than you and me. So what excuse do we have?

3. I'M SCARED TO FAIL

When someone says they're worried about starting something new because they'd fail, they don't understand that doing nothing is the greatest risk of them all.

Our own physical bodies and brains are great examples of this. When we stop moving our bodies or using our brains, they regress and shrink. We lose muscle power and memory functions. It's when we get out and move our bodies and use our brains that they become stronger and last longer.

Staying inactive doesn't mean you'll remain safely in the same place. It means you'll move backward. Yes, backward.

You can never escape absolute failure. It's impossible to live any life that's devoid of all risk. Every venture, every voyage, every idea, every movement has a level of risk. But with every risk you take, you open yourself up to bigger rewards and possibilities you may have never imagined earlier.

Failure only means you're trying and is, inherently, an indication that you're progressing. It shows that you're out in the arena fighting the battle and giving it your all.

If you think about it, failures are blessings in disguise if they teach you something, as they invariably do. They help you adjust course and get to the next stage with even more strength, knowledge, and skill than you had before.

Because of this, I have a hard time coming up with an occasion when I've "failed." Oh, I've fallen many times and even bruised myself badly, but

I've ever truly lost because it was that very setback that took me to the next step.

Remember, failing means you're moving forward. The next time you fall, don't feel ashamed. Get right back up, dust yourself off, and smile, knowing you're one step closer to success.

4. MY FRIENDS WILL JUDGE ME

Anyone who wants to do anything of significance will face their share of cynics, critics, and complainers.

Some people who judge you may have good intentions and genuinely care, but they'll hold you back from living the life you dream about. They'll project their own insecurities on you and squash your ambitions without even realizing the harm they're doing.

These people are only shouting out what their ancient amygdala brain is screaming at them: *Stay back! Don't step out! OMG, there just might be a saber-tooth tiger around the corner!* The problem with this argument is sabertooth tigers went extinct over 10,000 years ago. In our modern world, it's those who don't step out, educate themselves, figure out what they love to do, and go for it who get left behind.

As you move forward, some people in your life may discourage you from progressing. When you succeed, it makes them question their own quality of life, and that makes them uncomfortable, so they'll do whatever they can to pull you down and keep you at their level. They want you to remain where you are because that will give them permission to remain as they are.

You can only sympathize with such folk. Let them go on their own journey on their own time. In the meantime, distance yourself from them as much as possible.

Then, there are those who benefit from you playing small and will intentionally thwart your efforts. When you decide to change and follow your own heart, they'll lose whatever sacrifices or attention you make for them today. When you succeed, they'll lose that feeling of power by controlling your life and your destiny.

Watch out for these people, for they are toxic and destructive.

Finally, there are people who are simply envious and will say anything to bring others down to make themselves feel better. This includes people who spend an inordinate amount of their days criticizing other people's achievements. They get a short-term power kick out of being "the critic," but if you look close enough, you'll see they've not created anything in their lives and would not know how to even if they wanted to.

There is only one response to such folk, and that is to ignore them.

The sooner you remove these negative individuals from your life, the healthier you'll be and the happier you'll feel.

5. I'M NOT GOOD ENOUGH

When someone says they're not good enough, they mean they've no idea how capable they are or how far they can go.

The human capacity for knowledge, growth, and achievement is unlimited.

The only restrictions we have are the mental brakes we put on ourselves.

Please read those last two sentences again.

You won't understand how much you're capable of doing and what strengths you have until you begin to truly stretch yourself. Your capacity to do great things is greater than what you think it is today. This applies to all of us humans on earth. Yes, that includes you.

Believe in yourself and what you can achieve.

Your Rebel Plans

> *"Make it a rule of life never to regret and never to look back."*
> *Katherine Mansfield*

LIMITATIONS I PUT ON MYSELF

Take stock of where you are right now. Sit back and think of the biases that are holding you back from living the authentic life you desire to live.

Remember that famous quote by Henry Ford: "Whether you think you can, or you think you can't—you're right"? What things are you telling yourself you can't do? What blockades have you put in front of yourself or have allowed others to put for you?

Other than the five main limitations we went through, here are specific self-imposed barriers I've heard from the many women I've spoken to about this topic. Do you see yourself in any of these?

Age: I'm too young or I'm too old.

Time: I don't have the time or I'm too busy.

Knowledge: I don't know where to start or I'm not that smart to learn.

Self-Acceptance: Nobody cares about me, so why should I care about myself?

Relationships: My family or friends may not accept me if I change, and I'm scared they'll reject me.

Motivation: I feel lazy and I don't want to make any changes, or I gave up on my dreams a long time ago and I just don't care.

Internal Demands: I have responsibilities now (jobs, kids, spousal demands etc…), and I feel selfish even thinking about myself.

External Demands: My family or community will never allow me to follow my ambitions, and I live under their control.

Culture of Blame: I can't move ahead because of what happened in my past, because of where I am today, because of my parents, my background, the society, the government, etc.

Put down below the limitations you hold for yourself today. Next to each thought, write down the opposite of it, even if you don't believe it yet. Then, keep these in mind as you go through the remaining sections of this book.

Example:

My current limitation: I never remember anything.

The opposite of this: My memory is fantastic and I can remember almost everything.

1. A current limitation I have:

The opposite of this is:

2. A current limitation I have:

The opposite of this is:

3. A current limitation I have:

The opposite of this is:

4. A current limitation I have:

The opposite of this is:

5. A current limitation I have:

The opposite of this is:

Your Rebel Plans

"As long as you're honest, you have the opportunity to grow. It's when you shut down, go into denial, and try to start hiding things from yourself and others, that's when you lock in certain behaviors and attitudes that keep you stuck."
Tracy McMillan

EIGHT WAYS TO GET UNSTUCK

Before you go further, read the quote at the top of this page. Really ponder her message. However you feel about the quote or the author, know this: Tracy McMillan is speaking truth to power.

If we are to get unstuck and move forward with the changes we want in life, we've got to take a stand. We've got to take a stand with ourselves.

This means no more excuses. No more procrastination. No more hiding from the truth. No more following the same patterns and habits. No more pretending we're fine when we're hurting inside. And most importantly, no more blaming everyone else and their dog for how our lives have turned out.

These are all limitations that will keep you down and depressed in body, mind, and spirit. It's time to change this around and stand in your own power.

You may now think, "Okay, okay, I got it. But how in the heck do I get unstuck then?"

Let's look at eight specific ways you can unglue yourself from past beliefs, experiences and negative emotions holding you down so you can propel yourself to the life you dream about.

1. LEAVE THE PAST WHERE IT BELONGS

Two things. First, you are not your past. Second, what has happened in the past has happened in the past.

We don't have a time machine—at least at the moment this book was written—to go back and fix things. So there's truly no value in ruminating over what someone did to us or what we may have done ourselves.

If you're brooding over something negative you yourself did in the past, it's time to forgive yourself. There's no use berating yourself or harming yourself further. It's time to let go of whatever is bothering you and tell yourself gently to move on. If you realize what you did was not right, you've learned a valuable lesson.

Make a promise to yourself to never get in that situation again. Apologize if needed. Do this with kindness and love to yourself as well as those around you. Then, let go.

When we chew over what others did to us in the past, that burden remains on our shoulders, getting heavier and heavier the more we dwell on it. This seriously hinders us from getting ahead.

Yes, some of us have gone through difficult experiences that need to be talked about and wrung out of our system so we can feel free again. If these memories are especially traumatizing, you'll need help from a professional. Like many others, I've been there. You'll need to take the time to heal yourself and learn to take care of yourself again. This is crucial. But, as the wise old saying goes, time heals all wounds.

We need to be gentle with ourselves as we recover. Then, we need to let that go. If we don't, those negative emotions and thoughts will affect us as badly as if we're carrying twenty tons of bricks on our backs.

As a first step, make a conscious decision to let your past go, however hurtful or difficult it may have been. Then, sit quietly and breathe for a few minutes every day to train yourself to be in the now. Do this and little by little, you'll find yourself not dwelling on those unhelpful emotions and feelings anymore. It will take time, so be patient with yourself.

2. TRUST YOUR INSTINCTS

Listen to your gut.

You know when things aren't going the way you want, whether it's in a job, a relationship, or a commitment you made a while back. You know when you feel bad about something or when something just doesn't feel right. You know when you need to make a change.

Whenever you get that heavy feeling in the pit of your stomach, when you feel bad about what you're doing, who you've become, where you're hanging out, or who's surrounding you it's time to stop what you're doing. STOP. And take stock.

Set aside time to do some introspection by listening to your emotions and ask yourself why you feel this way.

We've all been there—when we've felt terrible about the circumstances we've found ourselves in. The reason we remain in these situations is because we're too scared to make the necessary changes and move away. But this is exactly when we need to move away. This is when we need to take a deep breath, find that ounce of courage within us, and ask ourselves if we want to remain where we are and continue doing what we're doing with the people we're doing it with.

It's not easy, but it's essential that you become aware of your instincts and take the time to do this self-discovery if you want to get unstuck. Next time your gut sends you red flags, pay close attention.

3. STOP STRIVING FOR PERFECTION

Perfectionism is a dream killer.

And a nasty one at that because many people walk around thinking it's noble to be a perfectionist. In reality, it's nothing but a barrier to your success.

Do you have a friend enrolled in their tenth class, program or conference in a row and still hasn't taken any meaningful action? Do you know of someone who has been revising a book for the thousandth time because they're too afraid to get it out and share their views with the world?

How many entrepreneurs tweak their business plans to the nth degree—I was one of them—before starting their business? It took me almost a year to realize this mistake. Things only took off after I took my first step—even if that meant I'd make a few mistakes.

"I am a perfectionist" is a great pretext to not change or move forward. Perfectionism is a crutch we can lean on, a pretty little excuse we tell ourselves and others to justify why we haven't done what we had set out to do.

You must learn to become comfortable with imperfection. You must explore, try and test even if it means you move only one inch at a time. The person who pushes away perfectionism and takes action is the one who'll get unstuck in life. They'll be the ones who'll progress while those trying to be perfect will stay where they are forever, tuning, tuning, tuning….

Think of that the next time you tell yourself that you're trying to make something perfect. "Perfect" simply does not exist.

4. GET OUT OF YOUR COMFORT ZONE

One of the easier ways to get unstuck fast is to change your routine.

This can be as simple as eating something you normally don't eat for breakfast, wearing a new piece of jewelry, or taking another path to your morning bus stop. You could go and say hello to the new guy or girl in your office. You could drive home from work through a new part of town and immerse yourself in a whole new cityscape.

While these activities may sound insignificant, they will trigger a sense of novelty in your mind. And this will make you more open to new ideas and ways of doing things—not drastically perhaps, but on a small scale nevertheless. It's a great way to start.

Now, if you really want to shake yourself out of your stuckness, you need to get bold. Do the things that send a tiny shiver of excitement running up your spine. Just remember that each of our thresholds for excitement and fear is different, so do what resonates with you.

You could take a public speaking seminar or take on a leadership role at a community club near you. You could volunteer at a non-profit organization or join your local softball or football team. You could go on a hike up a mountain you wouldn't have dared tried before or join a rock climbing club (make sure you get the proper training and guidance before trying these out). You could also take the train and spend a weekend as a tourist in a neighboring city. Or you could splurge and book a flight to a foreign land you've never been to before.

Your options are endless. And they don't have to cost you an arm and a leg.

When you're exposed to new activities in diverse places, your brain will go on alert as it tries to capture all the unfamiliar sounds, smells, sights and ideas. It will shake you up and force you to think differently. Even if you try the public speaking club for just one evening or rock climb for just one afternoon, it will get you out of your rut and make you see yourself and the world differently.

So, what new thing would you like to do to shake you out of your comfort zone?

5. FEEL THE FEAR BUT DO IT ANYWAY

Most people remain stuck where they are because they fear the future. They get anxious about what could happen, get mired in *what-if* thoughts, and quickly talk themselves out of progressing before they even begin.

Yes, considering the consequences of our decisions is a smart thing to do—in fact, we don't do this well enough sometimes. But we cannot get so immobilized by the fear of failure or the fear of success that we don't even take that first step.

No one can guarantee what tomorrow might bring. The future will always be uncertain. This is merely a fact of life. We need to learn to become comfortable being uncomfortable. We need to make decisions even when we don't have all the information or all the approvals or all the ____ (fill in the blank) ____ at our fingertips.

I share three decision-making tools for managing your fears so you can boldly step out into the unknown in *The Fear Buster*—a companion booklet to the Rebel Diva series. You can pick up your private copy for free here:

https://www.rebeldivas.com/rebel-plans-gift/

Look at the simple exercises in this booklet and use them whenever you face life's challenges or dilemmas and feel that frisson of fear come over you.

6. DELAY GRATIFICATION

Nothing worth having comes fast or easy.

Most people remain stuck because they chase the easy route. They fail to achieve what they desire because they run after quick and dirty solutions, then get frustrated and give up too soon, sliding back to where they were.

If you believe you are entitled to your life dreams, that they should fall into your lap without you lifting a finger, that's a surefire way to stay stuck where you are. You'll need to check your mindset here and ask yourself if this thinking is helping you or harming you.

If, however, you are ready to set goals, make a plan and follow through (which is what we will cover in this book), you'll work your way out of the mud and into a shiny new place. It will take grit, diligence, and perseverance on your part to achieve your dreams or anything in life for that matter. This doesn't mean that you won't streamline your processes and find efficiencies wherever you can. But without *staying power*, you'll fall back into the mud and remain there floundering.

Ask yourself if you're always seeking the quick and easy shortcut. Or if you hold the belief that you don't need to work to get what you want. If you do, rethink those beliefs, as they will hold you back in the long run.

7. TAKE THE FIRST STEP

Seth Godin said it best; "The way to get unstuck is to start down the wrong path, right now."

Take one step today. Write it down. Say it aloud to yourself if you must. Let others know. Hold yourself accountable. Then take the smallest action you can take to get out of your situation. You only need to take a baby step. The first step will motivate you to take the next one, then the next and the next. Before you know it, you'll be out of your muddy hole, cleaned up and moving onward and upward.

Feeling stuck is like any other emotion.

We can do something about feeling cold or hungry, can't we? Unless we live in abject poverty (and millions of people on this earth sadly do), most of us can find a blanket to cover ourselves up or a slice of bread to eat. In this same way, when we're feeling stuck, we can *do* something about that feeling.

Yes, that's much harder than throwing a blanket around your shoulders, but it's possible. The decision is yours. You can sit up and decide today to make the right choices to get yourself unstuck. Or you can rail against the world, make excuses, blame everyone else and continue to remain mired in the sticky stuff.

No one can pull you out of the muck but yourself. Not even a hundred horses. I can give you the harnesses, the ropes, the pulleys, or even a fifty-ton truck, but in the end, it's up to you to *decide* to grab the tools and use them for your own benefit.

If you're stewing over why you're still stuck, ask yourself if you have made the *decision* to not remain stuck yet. Then take your first step forward.

8. REMEMBER THAT LIFE'S TOO SHORT

In the first Rebel Diva book, *Your Rebel Dreams*, we talked about the shortness of our human lives. Yes, life spans are increasing with every new generation, but if you think about it, our journey on earth is still short. We go about our days with little thought or focus, and before we know it we'll have come to our end and wonder how it all slipped away.

Go back to that first book and do the life expectancy test in the Introduction section. Look at that number again—the years you have left on earth in a best-case scenario. Then, ask yourself if you're comfortable continuing the life you're leading right now. If this question elicits a "heck no!" from you, then for goodness' sake do something and make a change.

Dying with regrets is the worst hell you can put yourself through.

But you can avoid that if you start today. Decide today what you want the rest of your life to look like, be like, and feel like. Then, use the tools in this book or elsewhere to construct the life you dream about. Do it. Now.

YOU'RE ALREADY HALFWAY THERE

The good news is you're halfway there already.

If you did all the exercises in *Your Rebel Dreams*, you will have an amazing vision for yourself based on your fundamental values and personality traits. All you need to do now is to make it real. Using the tools and guidance in this second Rebel Diva book, you'll create a treasure map to get you to your dreams.

Take control of your future today!

"The way through a challenge is to get still and think about the next right move. And not be overwhelmed by it, because you know your life is bigger than that one moment."
Oprah

Here are seven questions to gain more clarity on where you may be stuck in life. Are you ready to do some introspection? Be honest with yourself here.

1. How frustrated am I about my life right now?

2. Which area in my life do I feel bad about the most?

3. Do I spend a lot of time dwelling and ruminating on these feelings of frustration?

Your Rebel Plans

4. What three specific habits do I have today that keep me stuck where I am? (Hint: excessive dwelling will be one.)

5. What do I fear about changing my life? What anxieties come to mind when I think of changing?

6. What excuses do I make for not changing my life around, for not taking one step forward?

7. No, really, what excuses do I give myself? How am I resisting change? Lay it all out so you can start working on them one by one.

"Live your life as you would climb a mountain. Climb steadily, slowly and surely. Every so often glance at the peak. Enjoy the scenery at every vantage point on the way up. Be prepared for all circumstances. Know that there is more than one way to the top. The magnificent view from the top is well worth the determination, perseverance and effort of the journey."
— Harold V. Melchert

DOING THE IMPOSSIBLE

Have you ever dreamed of climbing a mountain? Or have you already dared to climb one?

Though I live in North America now, I grew up in the far shadows of Kilimanjaro in East Africa, and have vowed to one day return to my childhood home and hike up that mountain. It's been a secret desire ever since I was a little girl, though I didn't know then how, when or if I'd ever be able to do it. This year, decades later, I finally put in place a budget and a plan and even wrangled a few friends to join me on this once-in-a-lifetime trip.

If you'd asked me about this climb a few years ago, I'd have dismissed it, saying, "But that's impossible." I'd have wondered how I'd get time off from work or find the money to fly halfway across the world, or if I'd embarrass myself by not being able to keep up with everyone else.

But then I remembered how I—the dorkiest college girl that ever existed (barely five feet, a gap in front teeth, eyebrows tweezed to nonexistence and that big 80s hair… and this was in the 90s), one with only a few dollars left for rent in her pocket—galvanized nineteen college mates, many of whom I didn't even know, to go skydiving. Yes, skydiving.

My university years had been busy. I spent my time trying to make friends and fit into a new country as a young immigrant. I worked several menial jobs to pay for tuition on top of tons of schoolwork. I built a new life in college.

At graduation though, with no family to speak of, I was terrified of leaving the campus environment that had now become my home. I was not prepared to go out into the "real world." The best way to make the transition easy—or so I thought—was to do something that would scare me even more. A solo parachute jump.

That sounds like a crazy idea, but it was what made the most sense to my foolhardy young mind. It was also my way to get out of my comfort zone and shake me out of my stuckness.

The problem, though, was while I'd conjured up what I'd wanted, I had no idea where to start. It took me several weeks to figure out that all I had to do was put my fears aside and set a goal. One with a specific timeline.

That made it easier for me to make a plan and take action, beginning with baby steps. While this is easier said than done, I followed this script of **goal-plan-action-reward** to finally get the results I was seeking.

One sunny Saturday afternoon, I jumped out of a perfectly functioning plane at three thousand feet in the air by myself, followed by nineteen college pals. I cannot put into words the exhilaration I felt that day. My heart still thumps wildly at the mere memory.

The best of it all? I learned that nothing is impossible if you put your mind to it. That one action initiated a series of decisions that propelled me forward in other areas of my life.

My current goal is not just to hike up Kilimanjaro, but to also raise funds for a girls' literacy organization that works on the ground. I don't want to make this climb about conquering a mountain or even my own fears. I want to make it all about giving value to others, especially those who may not have the opportunities I've been lucky to have.

I hope my climb will inspire young women who may have a hard time believing that those of us without physical prowess, the best looks, the biggest bank accounts or celebrity status can go after our dreams too. The funds I hope to raise will give back to the community by enabling young girls to stay in school. This is what gets me excited about this new dream of mine.

So, I set a goal, made a plan, and took action. Last year, I began a regular morning exercise routine, set up a "Kili Klimb" savings account where I stash a little money every month and made a list of people I can call on to support the cause. The goal is to do the climb a year from now. I'll update this book to tell you all about it so stay tuned, and if you'd like to join me on this expedition, drop me a line!

CLIMBING A MOUNTAIN

How do you feel about that big audacious vision you crafted in *Your Rebel Dreams*? Does it feel like an insurmountable mountain to climb?

Remember, humans have scaled almost every mountain on this planet, including the most treacherous summits, some many times over. Kilimanjaro's a Sunday walk in the park compared to these ranges. If we put our minds to something and believe in ourselves, we can do anything.

But a wish or a dream alone won't do. Successful mountaineers set goals and create a plan with the full climb in mind. They establish milestones, prepare, and train. Then, on the appointed day, they start with their first step.

While that first step is the hardest, they stay on track, check their progress, and remain tenacious. They know their route is made of many small steps like the first one. And they know each one counts. So as they climb, they focus on the next step, then the next, and the next.

They also know their climb is a marvelous undertaking few people get to do. So they stop to admire the breathtaking vistas at every turn. Their ultimate reward is the thrilling view from the top—the snow-covered peaks, the pristine glaciers, the sun shining between the jagged slopes of the surrounding range—and the intense joy flowing through their bodies like an electric current from knowing they achieved this feat.

Our lives can be fantastic adventures too if we climb to the top of the peak. We can plan and prepare for our lives with the long-term in mind. We can focus on each step and not forget to enjoy the beautiful views we see and the interesting people we meet as we go up.

Sadly, some folks sit at the feet of such majestic mountains not even realizing they exist. They bury themselves in mediocrity and merely survive each day.

Imagine if we lived our entire lives the way we'd climb a mountain. Just imagine how that would make us feel.

MOUNTAINS WE'VE ALREADY CLIMBED

You may not realize it or may have even forgotten, but you've already climbed a few mountains in your lifetime.

You may overlook previous experiences and consider them to be insignificant. But if you think back to the agonies you grappled with, the skills you had to tap into and the fears you had to overcome, you may well have climbed a few personal Everests by now.

We all have.

Some bigger mountains I've faced in my lifetime include coping with a difficult childhood, moving to a new city or country on my own half a dozen times, trying to make it as a penniless young immigrant, losing a job more than once, the devastating illness of a loved one, a divorce after a twelve-year relationship, the shock of a breast cancer scare, and more recently, diving into the uncertain seas of entrepreneurship.

After one climb, though, the next one became so much easier that I forgot how hard the first attempt had been. Sometimes I have to remind myself that I've survived this far. I have to tell myself that if I made it all the way here intact, I can surely persevere through anything my future brings. So can you!

Let's see if you can identify the mountains you've climbed so far.

Write down below the biggest and scariest moments you've faced in your life. Remind yourself how you overcame those hardships. Don't dismiss these important experiences because they are what makes you who you are today.

1.

2.

3.

4.

5.

Are you amazing or what?

Read this list again and again, and gain strength from it. Be proud of what you've conquered. You're a magnificent woman with so much more to give and receive in life. You are a Rebel Diva. Stand proud!

Your Rebel Plans

"You should never let your fears prevent you from doing what you know is right."
Aung San Suu Kyi

STUMBLES AND FALLS

During our travels through life, we may stumble or fall or take the wrong turn. This is inevitable, for we're not robotic machines but fallible humans liable to err from time to time.

The monumental mistake we can make when we encounter hardship is to stop and give up. Or worse, turn back. We'll never be able to enjoy the magnificent view from the peak if we do.

If, however, we get back up, dust ourselves off, learn from the fall, and keep on moving despite our bruises, we're sure to get to the top with a wide grin on our faces, those difficult parts of the trip a distant memory.

Remember, mistakes can be amazing opportunities disguised as failures if we only allow ourselves to open our eyes and see through the tears. Our ability to adjust to new situations and persevere through it all is key to our success in life. Acknowledging this simple fact will take you a powerful step closer to your vision.

STAYING AT THE BOTTOM

If, on the other hand, we lounge at the base of the mountain, never acting on our dreams because we're too frightened of falling, we'll end up in a banal cul-de-sac of life.

The worst part of this is we'll be forced to work to make other people's dreams come true.

Just to survive, we'll find jobs packing someone else's tent or bag or horse, or doing the grunt work to help yet another explorer go up. We'll stay behind and grudgingly watch as adventurer after adventurer comes down that mountain with shining eyes and brimming hearts, their lives forever changed.

I don't know about you, but I don't plan to bum around at the bottom. I plan to climb that mountain because it's in that journey that joy resides.

OUR COMPETITION

As we go through this once-in-a-lifetime trip called life, we've got to remind ourselves that we're not competing with anyone but ourselves.

So don't look back or sideways to spot other climbers. Keep your eyes ahead and move toward your own personal target.

This means not thinking about what other people say about you. Why waste precious energy and time on things you can't control? This also means not worrying about what others are doing or say they will do. Let them climb their own mountains on their own time. Wish them well and keep your eyes on your trail.

Here's one way I tackle any insecurities or fears I may have about what others are doing or saying. When I journal every night before bed, the first question I ask myself is this: What were my personal wins, and did I do better today than yesterday?

Most times I find areas of improvement. Sometimes it's as simple as the one extra push-up that morning or the ten minutes less I spent down social media rabbit holes. Other times it's as big as having written a thousand more words for my novel than the day before.

In this way, my focus is to compete with yesterday's me and no one else. I can move ahead without the risk of insecurity and self-doubt hanging overhead like a deadly avalanche ready to smother me out.

"Life-fulfilling work is never about the money -- when you feel true passion for something, you instinctively find ways to nurture it."
Eileen Fisher

OPPORTUNITY COST

For every mountain you climb, there will be others you'll have to choose not to climb. You'll always be giving up something to do the thing you want to do.

For example, if you're reading this book, you're not watching television or scrolling through social media. If you're watching television, you're not spending time with your family. Everything we do, whether it's brewing a cup of coffee or running for political office, will have an element of opportunity cost. This concept is neither bad nor good, but merely a fact of life.

Unless you clone yourself, there will always be only one you. Understanding your opportunity costs early on will reduce unnecessary regret or that sinking feeling in your tummy that you're sacrificing something.

The first step here is to acknowledge that we can only do one thing at a time. To do anything well, we must eliminate distractions, hone our craft, and execute our idea with all of our attention.

This means we need to think of the many available options in front of us—knowing we cannot identify everything—and then make a conscious decision to choose the one we want to pursue at this time. Having an open mind and being more self-aware at this planning stage will help you feel more settled and appreciative of the path you ultimately take.

So let's take stock of your opportunity costs.

Your Rebel Plans

What activities will you give up to pursue the Big Audacious Vision you've crafted for yourself? Examples could include watching television, playing golf, going on a summer vacation, upgrading your car or postponing buying a new home.

Be honest with yourself.

1.

Am I ready to sacrifice this one thing to achieve my vision? Yes / No

2.

Am I ready to sacrifice this one thing to achieve my vision? Yes / No

3.

Am I ready to sacrifice this one thing to achieve my vision? Yes / No

4.

Am I ready to sacrifice this one thing to achieve my vision? Yes / No

5.

Am I ready to sacrifice this one thing to achieve my vision? Yes / No

NOW WHAT?

Take a good look at your answers.

If you're feeling uncomfortable with what you've written, put this book away and sleep on it for a night or two. Ask yourself if your vision is worth not doing these other things. Enter your journey with your eyes wide open. Know what you're getting into.

Be brave and follow your dreams.

Your Rebel Plans

> *"When we do the best that we can, we never know what miracle is wrought in our life, or in the life of another."*
> — Helen Keller

ENJOY THE CLIMB

Once you get to the top of your personal mountain, you're sure to feel euphoric. You'll feel fantastic and amazed at the feat you've accomplished. But these feelings are temporary.

Most mountaineers say they don't stay on top of a peak for more than fifteen minutes. It's exciting to get up there, but inevitably, they have to come down and perhaps go scale another mountain.

How sweet would it be if you found rapture in each step up and each step down as well as being at the top? What if it's the journey that gives you the greatest bliss?

Climbing toward your vision doesn't have to be an arduous task. If you selected your vision based on your fundamental values, your inherent talents, and work you enjoy doing in an environment you love, your trip will feel like a treat.

Yes, you'll have to learn new skills and face challenges. Yes, you may make mistakes and need to course correct from time to time, but if this vision comes from your sweet spot, you won't feel drained. You won't give up halfway. The work you have to do will energize, embolden, and excite you.

This is why you started this adventure by identifying your values, flair, zone, and joy in the first workbook. When you have a solid understanding of these important facets to who you are, the path toward your vision becomes an amazingly pleasant one.

To be successful at anything, you need to relish the process of getting there. You need to find satisfaction in the journey itself.

If you want to publish a book, you've got to revel in the process of generating ideas, then sitting down and writing every single day. If you dream of running a marathon, you'll have to appreciate your daily training and workout regimen. If you plan to lead a non-profit organization, you'll have to love the process of managing a team and a budget, fundraising, and talking to sponsors.

It's those daily activities done with perseverance, grit, and joy that will lead you to success.

APPRECIATE YOUR WINS

As you embark on your life mission, you'll score wins both big and small. It's important to recognize these and reward yourself. To do this, you need to remain attentive to the results you're accomplishing.

Some people set goals, work hard, and achieve them, but move on immediately to the next big thing without acknowledging their successes. They give themselves neither the time nor space to feel jubilation for a job well done. This kind of living is only sustainable for a short while because they will eventually burn out, feeling like they achieved nothing.

Learn to appreciate your wins and celebrate them. After all, how many people have the gumption to go after their dreams as you have?

STAY MINDFUL

Here's one more thing you can do to sweeten the climb toward your vision.

Study after study has shown that staying mindful—being aware of every moment—increases our levels of satisfaction, regardless of what we're involved in. Paying attention to one task, one event, or one person at any one time helps us get in the flow. It keeps us engaged, makes us think sharper, and enables us to get more out of that interaction.

Psychologists say staying mindful is one of the healthiest mental practices we can adopt. It increases our productivity and the quality of our work, and even bolsters our happiness.

This remains true even if we're in an unpleasant situation, like being stuck in traffic or sitting in a dentist's chair. By staying in the moment, we can shut down anxieties about the future or ruminations of the past and focus on the present, acknowledging and accepting it. The compassion we feel for ourselves and others around us will increase, and we will respond intelligently rather than react in a knee-jerk fashion.

Author Eden Kozlowski said it best in an article on mindfulness she wrote for the *Huffington Post*: "Being mindful is like being a very calm sports announcer—being aware of the play-by-plays of life yet not getting too wrapped up."

If we can strive to become observers of our own lives, we'll get miles ahead in achieving our vision and find joy in the journey at the same time.

TEN TIPS

For your own good mental health, start practicing mindfulness today. Here are ten tips to help you begin:

1. Cut your ruminations. You can never bring back the past, so it's wasteful to stew over what has already happened. Catch yourself when you're mulling over the past and bring your mind back to the present.

2. Cut your worries. Worries are only projections of what might be, most of which may never happen. Like ruminations, catch yourself when you're feeling anxious and bring your mind back to the present.

3. Get outside and into nature. Go for a walk on the beach or in a park or the woods if you have access to natural habitats and immerse yourself with all of your senses when you're outside. Feel the breeze, listen to the leaves rustle and watch the birds fly above you. Staying

mindful while out in nature will do wonders for the good health of your body and mind.

4. Use each sense fully. Learn to savor what you see, hear, feel, smell, or taste, even if it's as simple as a breakfast plate of fruit in front of you.

5. Unitask, not multitask. We lose an astounding twenty minutes every time we jump from one activity to another. That's how long we need to refocus on what we were originally doing, so the smart thing to do is to stick to one thing at one time.

6. Pay attention. When you're working, turn off distractions and find the environment that allows you to focus best. This might mean turning off your phone or Wi-Fi or asking family or colleagues to not disturb you for the time you've allocated for an activity.

7. Schedule your work, then time your work. Use an online or paper calendar to plan your day and use alerts to help you stay focused and track your progress. Using a timer can increase your productivity as you know in the back of your mind the alarm will go off shortly, which will make you inevitably want to "beat the clock."

8. Learn to meditate. Spend ten minutes on a daily meditation practice if you can. Start with a couple of minutes a day and increase by one minute every day so you ease into it and make it a habit. You can use one of several guided meditation apps or tools to start. Headspace at www.headspace.com is one you may like.

9. Journal daily. Every evening before going to bed, write down your wins and what you felt grateful for that day. After doing this for a few weeks, you'll find that you're more aware of what you're thinking, observing, and doing throughout the day.

10. Remember to breathe. We breathe every single second. It's what keeps us alive. Whenever we find ourselves in a sticky situation, our breaths come fast and shallow. If instead, we take five purposeful deep breaths at stressful times, we'll be able to bring our minds back to the present and reduce our anxiety levels as we do so.

THE FIVE-SECOND RULE

Finally, apply the famous five-second rule. No, this is not the one that says you can safely pick up dropped food from the ground in a specific amount of time. This has more to do with your mindset and how long you'll allow it to dwell on the negative.

In her book, *The Five Second Rule: Transform Your Life, Work, and Confidence with Everyday Courage*, Mel Robbins, motivational guru extraordinaire, explains that it only takes five seconds to switch from unfocused ruminations to a positive, forward-moving action. According to her, it's up to us to choose our state of mind. If we stand up to our negative self-talk, we can become focused, worry-free, and highly productive.

Mindfulness is not only a healthy mindset to take with us on our journey toward our dreams, but it will also make the trip an enjoyable one.

From the list of mindfulness practices here, what are the top three ideas you'll try out this month?

1.

2.

3.

Your Rebel Plans

"It is impossible to live without failing at something, unless you live your life so cautiously that you might have not lived at all."
JK Rowling

FEAR OF FAILURE

What is failure but another name for progress, as long as we learn from it?

If you've never lost in life, that's a sign you're stagnant. It says you haven't tried anything substantial. It says you haven't put your skills, talents or passion to good use.

If you find yourself failing, it means you're doing something worthwhile, you're attempting something new, or you're trying to advance yourself. So take pride in your struggles, figure out what you need to learn from them, and promise yourself to move onward, no matter what.

When I look back over the years, it's my failures—from being put on probation in school, to having to scrounge my way cleaning toilets as a new immigrant, being let go from jobs, not getting the promotions I'd expected, and my sad divorce—that opened my eyes and taught me new life skills.

It was during those and other difficult times I made breakthroughs in my thinking and in my habits, so much so that in retrospect, I don't see them as failures at all. I wouldn't be where I am now if I hadn't had those difficult experiences. So I can only look at setbacks as opportunities to grow.

If you're feeling apprehensive about taking your first step toward your vision, here's a list of extraordinary women who've been tested many times, yet they persisted. They were determined to achieve success and weren't afraid to change direction or take detours if needed.

If they can do it, so can we.

❈ Amy Adams, among the highest-paid actresses globally, was terminated from three television shows in her early years.

- Vera Wang, who failed to make the US Olympic figure skating team, became an iconic fashion designer now in high demand around the world.
- Ellen DeGeneres, who was fired for being gay, went through so much bullying and rejection following her outing she endured years of depression. But she bounced back to host one of the most wildly popular global television shows.
- Beyoncé, who lost in a talent show in her youth—an experience she considers a defining moment that made her turn her life around—is now queen of pop.
- Arianna Huffington, who failed as a politician and got rejected by thirty-six publishers, created one of the largest global information platforms. She attributes her triumphs to her mother's wise words: "Failure is not the opposite of success but a stepping-stone to success."

So be brave. And remember to always fail forward.

FEAR OF SUCCESS

Just as some of us are afraid to fail, many of us fear success even more.

The thought of being responsible for what we're about to do, or being in the limelight where everyone can see and criticize us, can trigger powerful emotions that hold us back. It's important to recognize these beliefs and see their limitations, or we'll never take that first step.

Our only other option is to languish at the bottom of the mountain filled with regret, packing someone else's bag. Don't allow unnecessary worries to stop you from achieving greatness.

The most compelling message I've read on this topic comes from contemporary author and speaker, Marianne Williamson.

She says:

"Our deepest fear is not that we are inadequate. Our deepest fear is that we are powerful beyond measure. It is our light, not our darkness that most frightens us. We ask ourselves, 'Who am I to be brilliant, gorgeous, talented, fabulous?' Actually, who are you not to be? You are a child of the Universe. Your playing small does not serve the world. There is nothing enlightened about shrinking so that other people won't feel insecure around you. We are all meant to shine, as children do. We were born to make manifest the glory of the Universe that is within us. It's not just in some of us; it's in everyone. And as we let our own light shine, we unconsciously give other people permission to do the same. As we are liberated from our own fear, our presence automatically liberates others."

From: *A Return to Love: Reflections on the Principles of a Course in Miracles*

Amazing, isn't it? My favorite part of this quote is: "Your playing small does not serve the world."

It may feel presumptuous to think of us as "serving the world," but each and every one of us has an important role to play on this earth. I believe there's a reason we're all here. And that's to make full use of our intrinsic talents and passions and give to the world as much as we can before our time is up.

Given the odds of us being born are almost negligent (one in 400,000,000,000!), we should take no less an accountability.

Most of us reading this book are fortunate to live in a world of privilege with food on our tables, roofs over our heads, and the opportunity to hope and dream. Billions of women around the world live in dire circumstances, steeped in poverty and violence, hopeless for the future and unsure of what tomorrow will bring. They'd trade places with us in a heartbeat.

I sometimes wonder by what miracle was I born where I was and when. Was it a one-second difference that stopped me from being born in a dingy alleyway of a slum versus a family that had a proper home? What mysterious forces made me get born into one of the most exciting moments in human history where the entire world is exploding with so many opportunities? I'll probably never find out the answers to these questions (and you may think me crazy to even ask them), but there's one thing I know for sure. I'll always be grateful for everything I have today.

Given the absurd odds of our existence, is it not our responsibility to make the best use of all the gifts we've been given? Shouldn't we boldly push away our fears and march toward our dreams?

Terry Crews, an American actor and former football player who grew up in an abusive alcoholic family, has adopted a beautiful saying: "I exist to show others what's possible."

What if we all embodied this philosophy?

Think about the young girls and women in your life who may learn from you and be empowered by what you do. Our progress will not only enhance our lives but also the lives of those who watch, learn, and get inspired by us. Our success means we'll be able to thrust out a hand and pull up our fellow human beings.

They will get uplifted when we get uplifted.

"The biggest adventure you can take is to live the life of your dreams."
Oprah Winfrey

WHAT YOU'LL NEED FROM HERE ON

1. Keep an open mind.
2. Understand that you have choices.
3. Know that your possibilities are endless.
4. Believe in yourself.

. . . AND ENJOY THE PROCESS.

As you go through the exercises in this book, you may get some jump-outta-your-chair AHA moments. It may also take a few tries before you figure out some insights. Give yourself time and remember, there are no right answers.

The best results come when you respond instinctively. Let your heart speak. Listen to it with love and care, then write down what it says.

You make the best choices given the time and place you're at and the information you have at that moment. It's perfectly fine if you come back to this workbook a year later and see a different path. That's called growth.

WRITE IT DOWN

When you write things down, it gives you more clarity and focus, allows you to think bigger, helps you remember more, and gives you a greater chance of achieving what you want. Writing your thoughts down can even reduce the level of anxieties you face.

Use the white spaces in this book to write all your answers and ideas. You'll be thankful you did later on.

LET YOUR ANSWERS PERCOLATE

It's best to follow the topics as they appear, as skipping sections may not give you the full outcome you're looking for. For example, you need to clarify your goals before making a plan.

When completing this workbook myself, I found the best results came if, after doing one section, I let the ideas swirl around in my brain over a walk, my chores, or supper. Then, when I came back to the exercises, I had the answers I was looking for.

Give yourself time and take all the breaks suggested here.

Most importantly, let the process take its course and have fun with it.

WE'RE ALL UNIQUE

Remember, we're all different from each other.

One woman's life dream could be another's nightmare. Some of us may want to become songwriters or engineers while others may want to set up their own businesses. Others may dream of traveling the world with their family, seeing wonderful new things. None of these paths are intrinsically good or bad. They're just different.

Your goals are whatever *you* want them to be.

Comparing ourselves to the Joneses only kills our spirit. It's not only a useless venture but a crippling one. Diversity is what makes this world go around and besides, the seven billion of us can't possibly all want the same thing, can we? How boring would that be?

There's only one of you, and that's who we'll be focusing on and celebrating here.

"Don't be intimidated by what you don't know. That can be your greatest strength and ensure that you do things differently from everyone else."
Sara Blakely

OKAY LET'S RECAP THE REBEL DIVA BOOK 1

Before we dive into the exercises in *Your Rebel Plans*, let's go over what we explored in *Your Rebel Dreams*, book one of the Rebel Diva series.

CORE VALUES

In book one, you uncovered your fundamental values that drive your life's purpose. Go back to the first workbook and copy your core values below. This will help you keep them at the top of your mind as you go through the exercises in this book.

You don't have to have gone through *Your Rebel Dreams* to know this of yourself. If you have a good grasp of your foundational values, that's great. Let's get them down here.

Remember, these values form your inner compass, your personal guide in life. They can be especially handy when you face difficult options or big dilemmas. So whenever you feel unsure during any of the exercises here, flip back to this page and check your questions against these important values you hold within.

Your Rebel Plans

My Core Values are:

1.

2.

3.

4.

5.

"Build your own dreams, or someone else will hire you to build theirs."
Farrah Gray

MY SWEET SPOT

In book one, you also explored four significant areas of your life: your innate talents or the skills you can learn, the environment you desire to immerse yourself in, the work that brings you joy, and finally, the value or service you can offer to the world.

Let's go through these again to jog your memory.

My Flair - Flair is what you do well. These are your talents and what you're good at. This includes skills you've worked to improve, as well as what you're able and willing to learn.

My Joy - Joy comes from what you love doing. These are the things you adore tackling and what makes you jump out of bed in the morning, eager to start the day.

My Zone - Zone is the physical environment in which you live and work, the people you surround yourself with, and the information you listen to or watch and absorb every day.

My Service - Service is the value you give others or what you offer the world. This is how your talents and skills can fulfill others needs. This is where your purpose lies and where your why kicks in.

My Sweet Spot - Your sweet spot is where these four areas converge. This is where you should explore your passions. This is where you'll thrive in the long run.

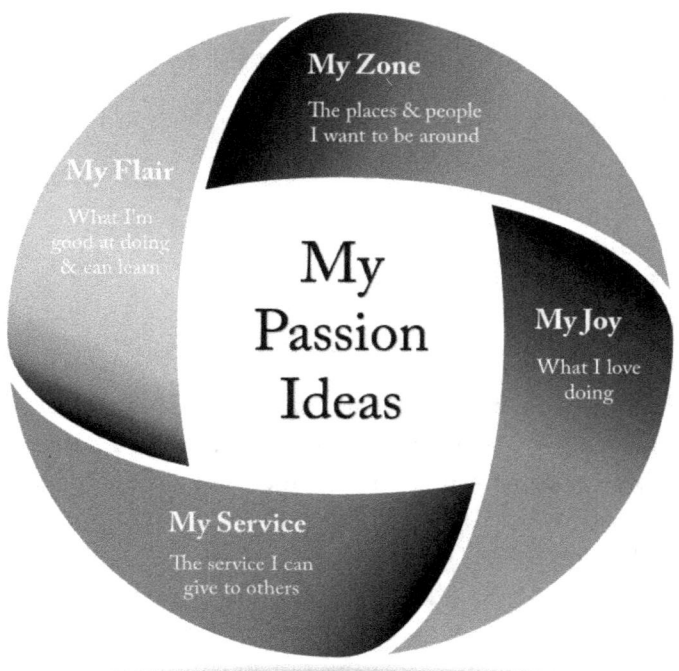

My Circle of Values

Life's too short to pursue anything other than what infatuates us. We can do things for money, fame, or other short-term gains and end up miserable with ourselves, or we can play in our sweet spot, feeding our passions, having the time of our lives.

If you did the work in the first workbook, you have a good idea of what this sweet spot holds for you. You'll have identified a few key passions that call out your name and chosen one passion idea—The One Thing—that resonates with you the most.

If you did the research suggested at the end of *Your Rebel Dreams*, you have tested your One Thing with colleagues, mentors, future employers, potential clients or customers in your field of interest. If you haven't yet, it might be a good idea to go back and look at the exercises in that workbook to see what you missed and where you may need to do more thinking.

Go back to the first workbook, and find the main passion idea you identified in your sweet spot, the one you want to work on this year. Now, write it down again here.

My One Thing - passion idea:

Your Rebel Plans

> *"Begin today. Declare out loud to the universe that you're willing to let go of struggle and eager to learn through joy."*
> *Sarah Ban Breathnach*

MAKE YOUR PLAN

We will go through these exercises in twenty-eight days.

That's four weeks for you to complete the sections, absorb the learnings, act on new ideas and finally come up with an action plan to make your big audacious vision a reality.

Schedule in one hour every Sunday for four weeks. That's it. All you need is just sixty minutes every Sunday afternoon or any other day that's quiet for you. Think of this as your *me-time*. Put it in your calendar and make sure others know you need to focus and not be interrupted.

I suggest you take a week off between each section to let the ideas, thoughts, and feelings marinate inside you. Then come back to this book the following week refreshed and ready to move on to the next section.

If you follow the itinerary suggested here, it will give you the time to get more clarity about what you want. You'll see through any fog that's built up in your life and ask the right questions to push through to the other side.

Here's your plan.

Week 1 Sunday

Date:	Complete Section One: My SMART Goals

Week 2 Sunday

Date:	Complete Section Two: My Execution Plan

Week 3 Sunday

Date:	Complete Section Three: My Check-ins

Week 4 Sunday

Date:	Complete Section Four: My Schedule

BREAK

Excellent work.

You've recapped your answers to the first workbook and have begun the thought process to create a treasure map for your big audacious vision.

It may feel like we're moving slow, but these steps are necessary to let your mind percolate with ideas before we delve into goal setting. We've covered opportunity cost, failure, successes, competition, mindfulness, risks, and uncertainty. That's a lot. Phew. You deserve a break.

Why not take the week off and come back next Sunday afternoon to start fresh?

Next up, we'll roll up our sleeves and establish your core goals.

While you're on your break, imagine what it will be like to live your vision. Then imagine what you might need to do to achieve it. Look at the vision board you created in book one. Think about the big steps you can take to get closer to this vision of yours.

Don't write anything down, just let your mind wander. Dream. Imagine. Let go and lose yourself in your thoughts. Then when you come back, you'll be ready to start the next section.

Enjoy your break. See you next week.

Your Rebel Plans

WEEK ONE

SECTION ONE SMART GOALS

What's my destination?

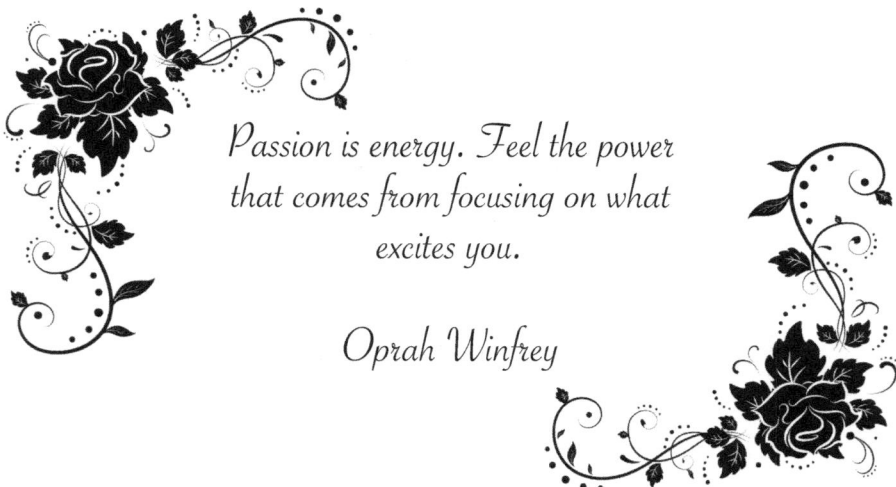

Passion is energy. Feel the power that comes from focusing on what excites you.

Oprah Winfrey

> *"The beginning is always today."*
> *Mary Wollstonecraft Shelley*

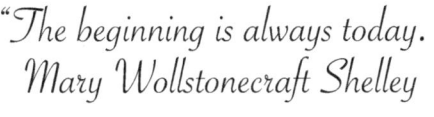

LET'S BEGIN

Have you got your one hour scheduled in? Have you told everyone this is your *me-time*?

Great.

Now, find a quiet and cozy spot to curl up in with this book, your favorite cup of tea, coffee, or beverage of choice, and a purple pen. Okay, you can use whatever color pen tickles your fancy, but I find purple ink always gives me a creative edge.

And that's all you need. Plus an open mind.

The journey to achieving your dreams is much easier than you think.

A SHORT MEDITATION

So, are you now in your favorite spot with a hot cup of tea, coffee, or maybe an ice tea?

Get comfy. Set your book down and put aside the cup and pen for a moment. Sit still with both feet on the ground, back straight but soft, arms to your sides, and your body relaxed but alert. Close your eyes.

Now, take five deep and slow breaths. Breathe in through your nose and out through your mouth. Feel your diaphragm expand and contract as you breathe deeply. Concentrate on your breath and feel it coming in and going out.

Make your breaths long and slow. Breathe in. And breathe out. Feel the air coming in through your nostrils and filling your insides. Then feel the whoosh of your breath as it leaves you. Keep breathing slowly, gently, mindfully.

Take your time and take as many deep breaths as you need to settle yourself. This will help you relax physically and clear your mind of any mental debris that could cloud your thinking. When you're done with the meditation, sit back and open up to the next page.

Answer the questions that show up, one by one. Be honest with yourself. Indulge in yourself. Put down responses that make you smile. You don't have to fill in all the blanks, only what you want.

You can start each section of this book with this short meditation to get you in the zone.

And remember you can and *should* celebrate every time you finish a section!

"Goals are my road map to the life I want. They have helped me accomplish things I once thought were impossible."
Catherine Pulsifer

YOUR NEXT STEP

You've come a long way in designing this thrilling new life of yours. By now, you've figured out your purpose and passions. You've identified your innate talents, your desired environment, work that brings you joy and the value you offer others.

Most importantly, you have a life vision you want to achieve.

But, visions don't come true simply because you write them down. They also don't materialize by wishing, hoping, or through osmosis. The introspection and writing down your vision were essential and key steps, but, you must take action for anything to happen.

"A vision without action is just a dream. An action without a vision just passes time. A vision with an action changes the world," said Nelson Mandela.

So, your vision is big and audacious. It's HUGE. Or at least, it should be. You might be looking at it right now with glazed eyes, wondering how you can ever take action toward something so significant. There is a way, and it's a simple and easy-to-follow method. Let me show you how.

BREAK THINGS DOWN

The trick is to dissect your vision using each step of the Passion Pyramid to come up with practical project phases (don't worry, we'll go through these soon). This way, your vision won't feel overwhelming and you'll have a series of logical actions to take, starting with your first baby step.

Here's what we'll do.

First, we'll derive your core goals from your vision. Then, we'll create an execution plan for your goals. Finally, we'll identify the specific action steps in this plan. By tackling each of these steps—the smallest denominator of this vision equation—you'll complete your plans, reach your goals and ultimately achieve your vision in no time.

BE FEARLESS

Your goals need to stretch you and even scare you a little.

They should never shock you out of following through, but they should give you a little jolt of happy electricity to remind you of the amazing journey you're taking.

When early explorers sailed to discover new lands, they didn't stop short of what they could see. Their goals were big and bold and they dared to think beyond what everyone else thought was literally the end of the world. These sailors of long ago were fearless in their actions.

Like them, let's make this life, the only one we'll probably ever have, a courageous one.

Don't strive to live a small life constrained by fear and doubt or encompassed by what you can see today or what others say. Think beyond your horizon. Ask yourself what treasures and adventures may lie out over there!

STAY FLEXIBLE

Now, I realize goal setting can be intimidating. For some of you, writing down specific objectives may feel like getting handcuffed. But remember, these goals you set are yours and yours alone. You can design them however you wish and you can always adjust them as you go along.

Just like the mountaineer who may spot a path to a peak with a better view and change direction, we need to stay agile. The hallmark of a successful person is their ability to adapt to new environments and pivot whenever they see new opportunities or when external forces show up and throw their plans awry.

The main reason for setting goals and making a plan is to have a roadmap so you know where you'll go and how you will get there. Without that outline, you could spend weeks, months or even years hitting dead ends, making U-turns, wasting energy, and not getting anywhere close to your vision.

We shouldn't think of setting goals as shackling ourselves. Having goals is actually freeing; it can spur us to action and help us get to our destination faster.

> *"Reach high, for stars lie hidden in your soul. Dream deep, for every dream precedes the goal."*
> *Pamela Vaull Starr*

So what does goal setting look like? Let me share an example with you.

AN EXAMPLE

Let's take Alice, a recently divorced single mother who's suddenly burdened with the full responsibility of taking care of herself and her young boy. The heartbreaking drama around the divorce is over, and she's left in the dust wondering what to do next. As with any life-changing experience, her mind goes in circles. She feels like she's about to implode and she asks herself how she ever got to this position.

She remembers the dreams she had as a little girl, dreams she'd given up for the promise of romance, 2.5 kids, a house with a white picket fence, the obligatory family SUV, and a golden retriever to go with it all.

Ever since Alice was a young girl, she loved to teach. She held pretend classes at home on weekends, subjecting her stuffed toys to her lessons. She dragged her mom's books out, put her dad's glasses on, and played teacher all day. Then, when she got older, she volunteered in summer camps as a guide and loved the feeling of igniting curiosity in other children and seeing them expand their thinking. She enjoyed being a mentor, someone others looked up to and learned from.

Now, as she stands alone in front of her kitchen window contemplating her uncertain future, she gives her head a shake, but that vision she revived is not going away that easily. It's only growing stronger inside her.

She'd always wanted to become a teacher, but she married early, had a kid, and settled for a low-level administrative position at the trucking company her ex-husband managed.

Your Rebel Plans

Is it too late to follow my dream? Her mind whirls. *Don't I need a year of teacher training on top of a degree for that? How can I afford to go back to school? Don't they say there aren't any teaching jobs in my city anymore? What am I thinking? I've got a kid to feed and rent to pay, on top of what I owe my divorce lawyer. I should just bury that dream….*

But wait.

Think about what Alice will teach her son if she shows him it's okay to live a small life. How remorseful will she be later in life if she doesn't take this opportunity to make her vision come true? Maybe there's a silver lining amid all the tumult she's experiencing. Maybe this is the perfect time to pursue her dreams.

What if Alice decides she wants to live a truly fulfilled life with no regrets? What if she goes for it?

Okay, what can she do next?

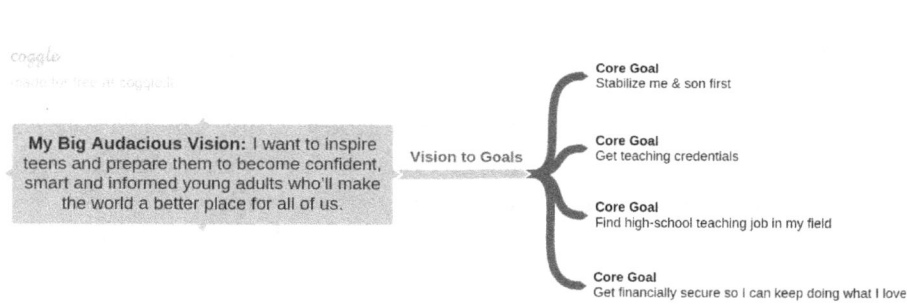

A GOAL MAP

It's especially in times of crisis or when life dilemmas show up that we need to pause for a moment, sit back and organize our thoughts. If Alice wants to explore her dream, her life vision, there is one tool she can use to logically and rationally think it out. And that is a goal map.

Generating your vision, as you did in the first workbook, was all about being creative, casting your idea net far and wide and reaching for the stars. Crafting your goal map and subsequent action plan (which we'll do together in this book) will need you to activate another part of your brain—the more analytical one that will make connections between the ideas floating in your head to come up with the practical steps you need to take to attain your amazing vision.

Let's look at what Alice did.

Here's the goal map she created to organize her thoughts logically.

She sat down in a quiet spot for an hour to think this through. She built this picture step by step to get a better idea about her vision and what it entails. At each step, she asked herself, "What does this mean? What do I need to do to get here?" Then, she worked backward.

ALICE'S VISION

Notice how Alice's vision is less focused on her personally and more on how she can help others—in this case, teens in school. You may think having a vision with intrinsic motivations like "I want to make a million dollars" would be much better. But study after study has shown that when your motivations lie outside yourself, the chances you'll achieve them are greater.

When you desire to help someone win through your actions, there's less chance you'll get discouraged by setbacks. And you'll have a greater probability of realizing that vision. So Alice was pretty smart to write her vision in this way.

Whatever vision you choose, you're sure to face a few obstacles on your path. When you make a commitment to others and you deeply desire to make your family, neighborhood, community or even the world a better place, there's little that will stop you. But you knew that already, didn't you?

ALICE'S CORE GOALS

Core goals are what you'll create using the exercises in this workbook. We'll get to yours in a minute, but let's examine Alice's first.

She has come up with four major phases or steps she needs to pursue to get to her vision. Some of these may happen in sequence or in parallel.

Some of them may need more time than others. We don't have to worry about such details at this stage. What's important is to identify the main steps needed to make the vision a reality.

Alice has come up with four sequential goals: first, get settled, then get the education, then find the right job, and finally create a brand-new career and life for herself and her son—all the while striving toward a vision where she'll be giving back to her community. She's followed a logical thought process. It's intelligent and rational as its compassionate.

ALICE'S SMART GOALS

Once you have a good idea of what your core goals are, you'll then need to translate them into SMART goals.

Using a simple formula (which I'll share with you shortly), Alice hashed out her core goals to better understand what they mean in terms of time, funds, and actions. This is how she gets practical about her vision. These SMART goals act as a series of torches that shine the path toward her future. Her road ahead is becoming increasingly clear.

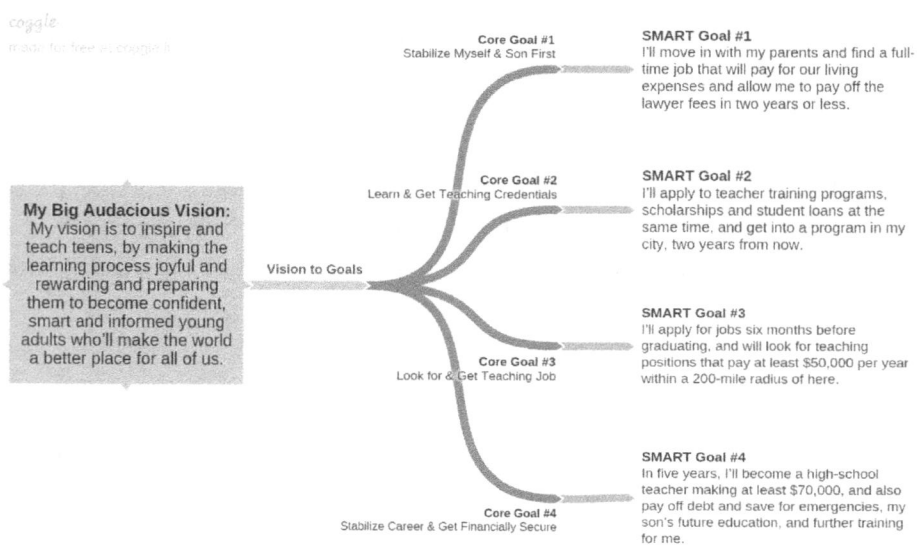

To create this, she used knowledge she already had and tapped into other people's experiences. She talked to her teacher-friends and mentors and read up on her area of interest (teaching teens) as much as she could. If you did the research exercise at the end of the first workbook, you'll have this information on hand and will be a step ahead of the curve.

If you haven't completed the first book, *Your Rebel Dreams*, this may be a good time to stop and go back to make sure you have all your ducks lined up before creating goals and action plans. Your journey will be easier and the path ahead clearer if you do.

Alice's dream is no longer a fuzzy pie in the sky. It's not a mere wish or hope, but something she can conceptualize and work toward. Now, this may not be the perfect path, nor will it be free of roadblocks. But she has a powerful light shining the road ahead and she can take her first step forward.

And this is an empowering place to be. We'll get you there too, very soon.

MIND MAPPING TOOL

There are many ways to illustrate this process. The best way I've found is to create a mind map, which is what you see Alice did here.

With a mind map, you take a big idea and chunk it down to the smaller steps without worrying about details or even how accurate it is (you can adjust this later on). You're thinking big at this point.

From here, you'll branch down and add more specific information to clarify your path. Your mind map can have as many branches as it needs, depending on the complexity and size of your vision. The important thing is to make sure the logic follows through as you move from the larger branch to the smaller ones.

You can use a pen and paper to draw this picture or try any of the mind-mapping software available online. I like Coggle because it's easy to use and free. You can find it at www.Coggle.it.

While it may seem like upfront work, creating this map will pay dividends for years to come. You need to create this only once and adjust it every year, and only if needed.

We can use this model to create a plan to become a plumber, a doctor, a baker, or a head of state. What you put in these plans is entirely up to you. A goal map will steer you in the right direction, but there's another side benefit to having one. Looking at it every day can give you a sense of purpose and hope. You'll realize that any drudgery you face today is temporary. You'll wake up knowing though all may not be great at the moment, you're working toward a bigger vision, one that will benefit you and your family.

That will propel you to do the things you need to do to get to your vision. Now let's go create this goal map for you.

> *"Some women choose to follow men, and some women choose to follow their dreams. If you're wondering which way to go, remember that your career will never wake up and tell you that it doesn't love you anymore."*
> *Lady Gaga*

Copy your big audacious vision here.

I know, I know. I keep asking you to write your vision in every section. That's because repeating this practice will ingrain it further in your mind and increase your conviction in your future and in yourself every time.

My Big Audacious Vision:

```
┌─────────────────────────────────────────────┐
│                                             │
│                                             │
│                                             │
│                                             │
└─────────────────────────────────────────────┘
```

BE COMFORTABLE WITH UNCERTAINTY

If you're asking yourself whether your vision is even attainable, that's not a bad thing. It means you're stretching yourself, which will require you to think big, learn new skills, meet new people, and expand your perspective. All of this will open doors you may not even realize exist. If you already have a clear idea of how to achieve your vision, you're not dreaming big enough.

Alice wasn't certain about every detail when she designed her goal map.

She didn't know if they'd accept her to any teacher training college or whether there'd be jobs when she graduates. She's also grappling with finding a new place to live and taking care of a child who's going through his own issues after seeing his parents split up. She'll take as much time as she needs and plow through her plan, trusting the answers will come. She's also aware that she needs to remain vigilant and be flexible if she learns she's better off going in an entirely new direction.

So don't worry if you don't have the entire path fully laid out in front of you and you're feeling a little scared right now. When you're playing with a big idea like your vision, you must become comfortable with any feelings of uncertainty.

CORE GOALS

Take a look at your vision and think of the most high-level and maybe even improbable (for now) steps you need to take to get to it. Break your vision into three to five chunks and draw up the first set of branches of your goal map.

You can brainstorm this in several ways, but the easiest is to look at the main stages of work you need to complete if you want to reach your vision. Look at sequential phases (first, do this, then do that, next do this, etc....) to get the ball rolling.

BRAINSTORMING

Since Alice did the research suggested in the first workbook, *Your Rebel Dreams*, she has the preliminary information to start. She's spoken to other teachers and researched college programs to learn more about their teaching curricula. She's even had a chat with an old mentor from high school to clarify her career idea further.

In the same way, go back to the first book and look at the answers you gave to those final questions in that book. Did you speak to your friends, colleagues, potential employers, or clients about your passion idea? Did you root around the Internet and research your field of interest? If you have, this exercise shouldn't be that difficult. You'll already have several clues for what your core goals should look like.

If this task feels slightly overwhelming, this is a perfect time to speak with a trusted mentor or bring a few good friends over for wine or tea and brainstorm together, so you'll benefit from their suggestions. You don't have to use all of their ideas, but pick the ones that make sense to you and resonate with you the most.

If you do this, be discerning about who you invite in.

HOW MANY GOALS ARE BEST?

There is no perfect number of core goals to have. The number will depend on the magnitude and complexity of your vision and how courageous you feel.

The core goals you set at first may not get you to your vision as directly or as fast as you expect, especially if you're dreaming big (which you really should be doing). These goals can form your preliminary foray into your journey. A year down the road, you can reevaluate and set the next level of core goals. This way, you get to your vision in phases.

As they say, Rome wasn't built in a day. You'll need to be patient with yourself and your dream.

I like to stick with three to four goals. I make sure they'll stretch me without creating undue pressure throughout the year.

Make sure what you come up with is manageable and doesn't paralyze you into inaction. If all you can focus on next year is ONE big goal which you're certain you'll work on, that's better than having a big plan with several goals you won't touch.

Remember, there are many paths to your life vision, so there's no need to restrict yourself to only one. If one fails, you can always try another. You'll always have options.

Your Rebel Plans

STAY AWAY FROM THE WEEDS...FOR NOW

In the remainder of this section, you'll convert your core goals into SMART goals, which will be the basis for your execution plan. It's that execution plan that will tell you what exactly you need to do next. This is where you'll get really specific and weed out what's doable from what's not.

If you think in too defined terms at this core goal-setting stage, you'll restrict yourself. You may miss out on some wonderful ideas you want to pursue and that you're perfectly capable of achieving.

So let's get your core goals lined up to meet the big audacious vision you've crafted. Without worrying about their practicalities, brainstorm the big steps you need to take to achieve your vision. These will be your core goals. And refer back to Alice's goals if you get stuck.

My core goals are:

1.

2.

3.

4.

5.

"It's about being alive and feisty and not sitting down and shutting up even though people would like you to."
Pink

SMART GOALS

Smart gals need smart goals, so let's get on to making your core goals SMART.

The SMART goal method is considered best practice in almost every industry and has served me well in both my corporate and personal worlds. Here's that system, but with a twist.

A SMART goal has five main components: specific, measurable, actionable, rewarding and time-bound. Let's break this down:

SMART	What This Stands For	What This Means
S	**Specific**	Your goals are at a high level, but they need to state your desired outcome to help you visualize what you're after. Make it specific enough that when you read it out loud—which is something you need to do every day—you can see it in your mind's eye and feel a tingle in your bones as if you've already achieved it.
M	**Measurable**	"What gets measured gets done" is a common saying in the business world, but we can apply this to our personal lives as well. We need to write down our goals in a way that makes it easy for us to check against them so we know when we're done and how well we did. Tracking your goals is a surefire way to keeping them alive and from my experience, it's what will expedite the journey.

A*	Actionable	You need to glean your next steps from your goals. This is where you can break down your big goals further. Instead of rejecting a goal because it doesn't seem realistic or feels too big right now, see if you can phase it out, move it to next year, or break it into two or three smaller goals. Don't throw away your dreams. Make the system work for you.
R*	Rewarding	Your goals should be objectives you work toward joyfully. If you're going to set goals, why pick second-rate stuff? Why not create goals that raise goose bumps on your arms and make you grin to yourself when no one's looking? Go for what you really, really want.
T	Time-bound	To make a goal work, you must give it a time frame. A deadline gives traction to your work. Otherwise, your goals may remain nice-to-have-dreams for someday. Remember "someday" doesn't exist on our calendars. So, put solid dates down. Keep in mind these aren't set in stone, but they will guide your planning.

*Changed from the original methodology.

DO WE STRIVE FOR REALISTIC?

Here's the twist I mentioned earlier. The letters A and R in SMART are generally used to denote "Achievable" and "Realistic," but I chose different words for our big audacious visions.

Words like *achievable* and *realistic* are limiting. If all the great goals in the world had been realistic or easily achievable, we'd never have discovered electricity, designed airplanes, explored the moon, or conceived of the Internet. We'd never have overcome slavery in America or accomplished what we have for women's rights around the world today.

Why not stretch ourselves? This is not the time to play small or timid. This is the time to think big. Life's too short to do otherwise.

If you don't believe this, go back to the first book, *Your Rebel Dreams*, and redo the exercise on your life expectancy. And while you're at it, reread the top five deathbed regrets. Let me share that list again in case you've forgotten.

1. I wish I'd had the courage to live a life true to myself, not the life others expected of me.
2. I wish I hadn't worked so hard.
3. I wish I'd had the courage to express my feelings.
4. I wish I had stayed in touch with my friends.
5. I wish I had let myself be happier.

From *The Top Five Regrets of the Dying* by Bronnie Ware

So, do you still want to play humble with the only life you've got?

BANISH PERFECTION

In the beginning, you may find some of your goals don't have all of their SMART components. And that's fine.

The most important thing is you've started climbing toward your vision. Your goals will get refined as you learn more about yourself and your path ahead. If you wait for the perfect goals and plans and timing, you'll never get started, let alone achieve your vision.

Think of your journey as a car on a road trip.

When the car is stopped on the side of the road with the engine turned off, you can't change direction or do much of anything. But once you start the engine, pull onto the road, and roll, you can turn the wheels at any time (as long as it's safe to do so). You can change direction if you took the wrong turn or make a U-turn if you're heading away from your destination. You can even speed up or slow down as needed.

Starting the engine and taking that first move is crucial. Otherwise, you'll remain stuck on the side of the road forever, dreaming about your destination, but with no power to get there.

So start, anyhow.

PRINT EXERCISES IN BOOK

Don't forget to download the PDF worksheet booklet for *Your Rebel Plans*.

This 100+ page booklet includes worksheets for all the exercises in this book. You can print them, write your answers directly on them, pin them up if you'd like and refer to them every day.

Go to the link below to download your free private copy.

Your Rebel Plans Worksheet Booklet

(https://www.rebeldivas.com/rebel-plans-gift/)

Your Rebel Plans

> *"You have to imagine it is possible before you can see something. You can have the evidence right in front of you, but if you can't imagine something that has never existed before, it's impossible."*
> Rita Dove

Rewrite your vision here so it stays at the top of your mind as you hash out your goal.

My Big Audacious Vision:

MY GOALS - QUESTION 1

In the table on the next page, write down the SMART components of your first goal. Think through each of the questions below and write your answers down. No need to make this look nice. Put bullet points. Sketch a drawing if that helps. Capture the gist here and you can pretty it up later.

Your Rebel Plans

GOAL 1

(S) Specific	(M) Measurable	(A) Actionable	(R) Rewarding	(T) Time-bound
What specific outcome will come from this goal?	How will I know I've achieved this goal?	What main actions do I need to take to achieve this goal?*	How rewarding and enjoyable will the work and the final result be for me?	When do I want to achieve this goal by?

* We'll work on this more in the next section, so keep it high-level.

Using the notes you scribbled above, condense your goal #1 into one short sentence. You can use the examples I gave previously for Alice to craft your own.

SMART GOAL 1

By _____, 20_____, I will:

How I will *feel* when I've met this goal:

> *"Every moment wasted looking back keeps us from moving forward."*
> *Hillary Clinton*

Rewrite your vision here so it stays at the top of your mind as you hash out your goal.

My Big Audacious Vision:

MY GOALS - QUESTION 2

In the table on the next page, write down the SMART components of your second goal. Think through each of the questions below and write your answers down. No need to make this look nice. Put bullet points. Sketch a drawing if that helps. Capture the gist here and you can pretty it up later.

Your Rebel Plans

GOAL 2

(S) Specific What specific outcome will come from this goal?	(M) Measurable How will I know I've achieved this goal?	(A) Actionable What main actions do I need to take to achieve this goal?*	(R) Rewarding How rewarding and enjoyable will the work and the final result be for me?	(T) Time-bound When do I want to achieve this goal by?

* We'll work on this more in the next section, so keep it high-level.

Using the notes you scribbled above, condense your goal #2 into one short sentence. You can use the examples I gave previously for Alice to craft your own.

SMART GOAL 2

By _____, 20_____, I will:

How I will *feel* when I've met this goal:

"Nothing is impossible. The word itself says I'm possible."
Audrey Hepburn

Rewrite your vision here so it stays at the top of your mind as you hash out your goal.

My Big Audacious Vision:

MY GOALS - QUESTION 3

In the table on the next page, write down the SMART components of your third goal. Think through each of the questions below and write your answers down. No need to make this look nice. Put bullet points. Sketch a drawing if that helps. Capture the gist here and you can pretty it up later.

Your Rebel Plans

GOAL 3

(S) **Specific** What specific outcome will come from this goal?	(M) **Measurable** How will I know I've achieved this goal?	(A) **Actionable** What main actions do I need to take to achieve this goal?*	(R) **Rewarding** How rewarding and enjoyable will the work and the final result be for me?	(T) **Time-bound** When do I want to achieve this goal by?

* We'll work on this more in the next section, so keep it high-level.

Using the notes you scribbled above, condense your goal #3 into one short sentence. You can use the examples I gave previously for Alice to craft your own.

SMART GOAL 3

By _____, 20_____, I will:

How I will *feel* when I've met this goal:

> *"I am no bird. And no net ensnares me. I am a free human being with an independent will."*
> Charlotte Bronte

Rewrite your vision here so it stays at the top of your mind as you hash out your goal.

My Big Audacious Vision:

MY GOALS - QUESTION 4

In the table on the next page, write down the SMART components of your fourth goal. Think through each of the questions below and write your answers down. No need to make this look nice. Put bullet points. Sketch a drawing if that helps. Capture the gist here and you can pretty it up later.

Your Rebel Plans

GOAL 4

(S) Specific What specific outcome will come from this goal?	(M) Measurable How will I know I've achieved this goal?	(A) Actionable What main actions do I need to take to achieve this goal?*	(R) Rewarding How rewarding and enjoyable will the work and the final result be for me?	(T) Time-bound When do I want to achieve this goal by?

* We'll work on this more in the next section, so keep it high-level.

Using the notes you scribbled above, condense your goal #4 into one short sentence. You can use the examples I gave previously for Alice to craft your own.

SMART GOAL 4

By _____, 20_____, I will:

How I will *feel* when I've met this goal:

"Whether you come from a council estate or a country estate, your success will be determined by your own confidence and fortitude."
Michelle Obama

Rewrite your vision here so it stays at the top of your mind as you hash out your goal.

My Big Audacious Vision:

MY GOALS - QUESTION 5
COMPLETE ONLY AS NECESSARY

In the table on the next page, write down the SMART components of your fifth goal. Think through each of the questions below and write your answers down. No need to make this look nice. Put bullet points. Sketch a drawing if that helps. Capture the gist here and you can pretty it up later.

GOAL 5

(S) Specific	(M) Measurable	(A) Actionable	(R) Rewarding	(T) Time-bound
What specific outcome will come from this goal?	How will I know I've achieved this goal?	What main actions do I need to take to achieve this goal?*	How rewarding and enjoyable will the work and the final result be for me?	When do I want to achieve this goal by?

* We'll work on this more in the next section, so keep it high-level.

Using the notes you scribbled above, condense your goal #5 into one short sentence. You can use the examples I gave previously for Alice to craft your own.

SMART GOAL 5

By _____, 20_____, I will:

How I will *feel* when I've met this goal:

"People respond well to those that are sure of what they want."
Anna Wintour

PUTTING IT ALL TOGETHER

To see all of your goals together and to further ingrain these in your mind, rewrite them here. You can either list them here or put them into the goal map diagram. Choose what works best for you.

SMART GOAL 1

By _____, 20_____, I will:

SMART GOAL 2

By _____, 20_____, I will:

SMART GOAL 3

By _____, 20_____, I will:

SMART GOAL 4

By _____, 20_____, I will:

SMART GOAL 5

By _____, 20_____, I will:

THE GOAL MAP

On the next page is the goal map template with the extra branch for the SMART goals included.

See if you can fill in the blanks here and complete this picture. Go to Coggle.it to create this for yourself, or print this page and write on the image itself, or just scribble it down on a piece of blank paper or a whiteboard—whatever works best for you.

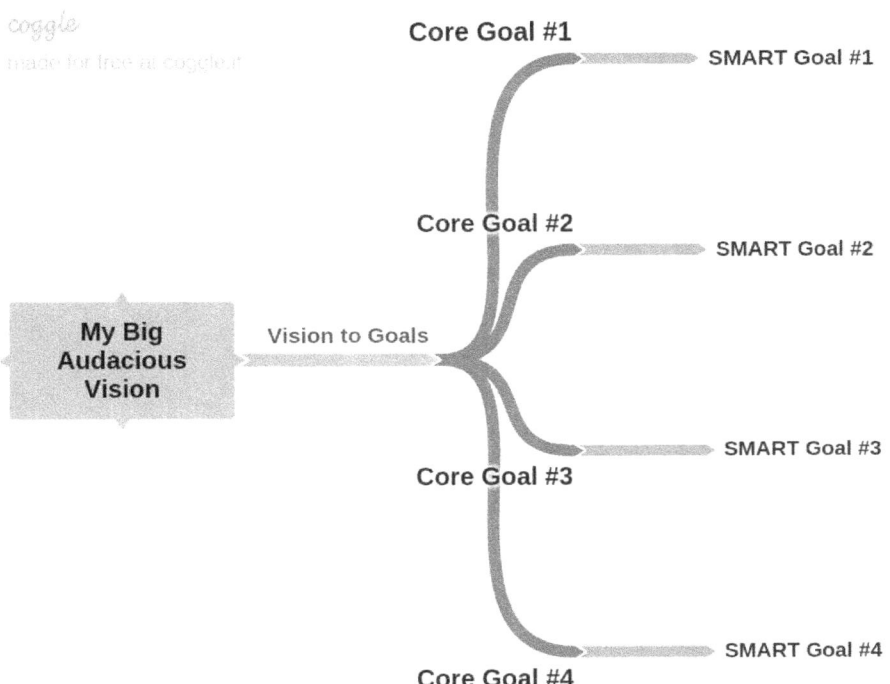

Your Rebel Plans

"As soon as I accomplish one thing, I just set a higher goal. That's how I've gotten to where I am."
Beyoncé

ANOTHER EXAMPLE

Let me show how this planning process can work in any field, even where there are no rules to follow or no road paved ahead.

Here's my current goal map. I share this to show how you can deal with fear and ambiguity, especially for larger-than-life visions.

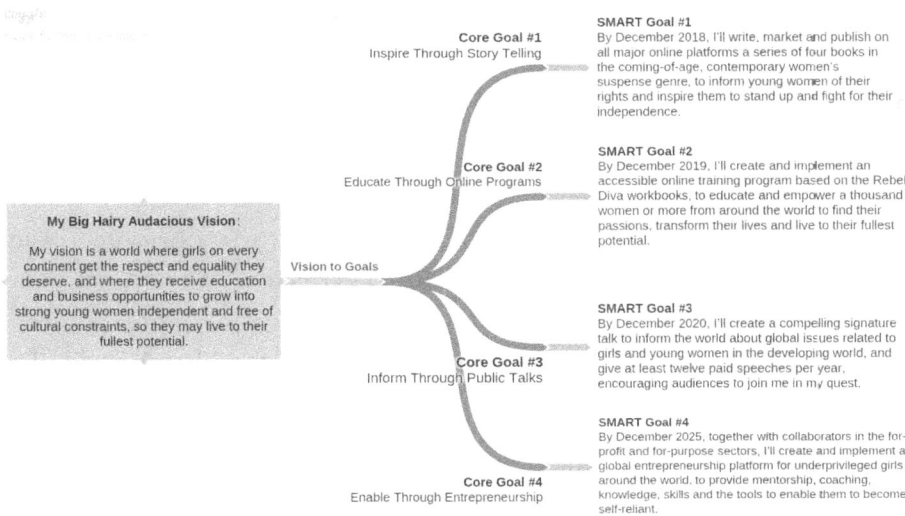

SMART CRITERIA CHECK

S - All the goals here, except the last one, are as **specific** as high-level goals can be. I can visualize them and imagine what the result will look like.

M - All except the last goal are **measurable**. I can track them by various indicators, for example, the volume of books published, the number of subscribers to a program, or the amount of talks given per year.

A - I can derive specific **action** items from all the goals here except for that last one. Actions could include writing books, creating courses or programs and planning talks, among others.

R - All these goals are highly **rewarding** for me and are based on my personal values. Just saying these goals out loud raises goose bumps on my arms and makes me ecstatic about the path I've chosen.

T - Finally, all these goals have a specific **timeline** so I know what dates I need to work toward.

Now about that goal #4.

This final goal needs more polish. I share it with you because I want to show a work in progress where I ignored perfection and wrote it down anyway.

This goal is much bigger than the others so I may need to phase it out or break it down further. To tell the truth, this goal frightens me a bit.

When I look at it, my mind swirls with thoughts like, *Who am I to dream like this? Where do I even start? What if I fail so massively and everyone laughs at me?* Then, another part of me stirs awake and asks, *But what kind of life am I going to live if I don't give it a go? Who cares what others say; isn't this my life to live? What's wrong with trying and seeing where this will take me?*

I know this goal is something I really, really want to achieve, but I'm not exactly sure how or what the final product will look like. However, I'm confident I'll figure it out as I talk to more people and as I work toward my other goals.

It's only a matter of time. Exploring this goal further is part of the journey.

✽✽✽

This vision may sound lofty, and I'm aware I'll not achieve this alone. I'm also not sure if the core goals listed here are enough to get me to my vision. Like any climber, I know I'll face uncertainties and risks. But I also know my greatest failure will be not to strive toward my vision at all.

So I've decided to dream big even if it scares the heck out of me. I'll carry on even if people mock me.

From here on, I must stay flexible and remain patient. I'll have to try new ideas, learn new things, and pivot when necessary. I'll need to connect and collaborate with people who have the same passions as me. I'll have to give it my best and remember to enjoy the adventure.

SO, HOW DO YOU FEEL?

That's the end of this section. Write down anything that wasn't captured in the questions but that you want to get out of your system.

1. How do you feel after completing this section?

- ○ Meh. Nothing interesting here
- ○ I really want to get this, but I'm lost and need help
- ○ I'm doing well. Just need to think some more
- ○ Fantastic. I've nailed this round. Woo-hoo!
- ○ Other: _____

2. What do you still need to figure out?

A.

B.

C.

3. What actions will you take in the next seven days to keep this topic on the top of your mind and clarify it further?

A.

B.

C.

BREAK

Awesome work. Remember, we're not looking for perfection. We're looking to start rolling, and you already have. Hurray! It's time for a well-deserved break.

They say innovation happens when ideas have sex. As weird as it sounds, let your goals have sex in your head while you go about doing everyday things. Let your ideas and thoughts swish around your brain, then come back next Sunday afternoon when you have another sixty minutes of relaxed me-time to start the next step toward your life vision.

Enjoy your break. See you next week.

Your Rebel Plans

WEEK TWO
SECTION TWO EXECUTION PLAN

How do I get to my destination?

Nothing will work unless you do.

Maya Angelou

"Teach your daughters to worry less about fitting into glass slippers and more about shattering glass ceilings."
Melissa Marchionna

THE EXECUTION PLAN

Okay, so you have your SMART goals hashed out. So what do you do next?

Your next step is to create an execution plan. When you have this execution plan in place, you'll know specifically what your next action will be. And you won't feel you're trying to eat an elephant in one big bite (I'd never eat a poor elephant, but you know what I mean).

Just like you broke down your big audacious vision into core goals, you'll break down each of your SMART goals into action plans. These action plans will detail the **what, when, where, how, by whom, with whom, and at what cost**. This is where you'll be asking hands-on, practical questions about how to attain each of your goals.

These individual action plans you develop per goal will together form your overall execution plan. It's this execution plan that will navigate you toward your overarching vision. This will be your treasure map for your vision.

You still must keep your eyes open in case the terrain changes. You'll need to stay flexible should you discover new trails or learn of better paths, but you'll have a map in your hands that will show you the direction you need to climb.

Don't worry. I have a template to help you create it here.

※※※

Before we get to your execution plan, here are a few things to clarify so you're set for success.

SCHEDULE YOUR TIME

You're probably wondering by now, with all this visioning, goal setting, and now planning, *where in god's name do I find the time to do all this?*

First, you shouldn't be dabbling with your values. If you've figured these out once, they may remain true for a lifetime or at least a decade or two, until you go through another transformation in your life.

If you're fiddling with your values, you need to go back to the first book, take a hard look at the questions in there. Then dig deep within yourself to understand who you truly are before continuing with any goals or plans. This is crucial. If you don't know who you are and where you are now, how can you figure out where you're going?

The vision you crafted is for the long-term and will be your true North Star for years to come. It's not something you play with unless it wasn't a serious one in the first place.

Goal setting and planning are activities you do once a year at the most. This is when you put all those ideas swirling in your head into a logical and rational picture and translate them into actionable steps—steps that will ultimately get you to your vision.

You can do this at the beginning of every year. Set aside a quiet weekend in January to take stock of the past twelve months and look at the year ahead. Taking a few hours to create a plan that will guide you for the rest of the year is time well spent.

Once you go through these Rebel Diva workbooks the first time, you'll have undertaken the most challenging work. You'll have done the introspection and self-reflection. You'll have a clear idea of your fundamental values and passions. You'll have learned the ins and outs of structured goal setting and how to create an execution plan. After that, making adjustments and improvements will get easier and faster every year.

You'll tinker less with the structure of your goals and the words in your plans and spend more time thinking of the bigger questions related to where you're going in life. It's hard not to develop a taste for personal planning when you see the progress you're making.

It will (hopefully) become so enjoyable that you'll look forward to planning every year.

THE POWER OF A PLAN

Similar to how you can move a car that's already in motion with a slight flick of your wrist, it's much easier to change course once you start rolling with your execution plan.

These plans you create won't be perfect. No plan ever is.

The military has an infamous saying that *no plan survives contact with the enemy.* Does this mean that the Army, Navy, or Air Force merely shrug their shoulders and run around doing whatever and whenever?

No, they plan, and they plan extremely well, possibly better than any other sector on Earth. I know because I've worked in their planning departments and have seen firsthand what they're capable of.

Plans may never be perfect, but without them, you'll be blind to your options, leaving you unsure of which direction to turn.

Without plans, most people end up going nowhere. They stay stuck in their original position and become victims of whatever life throws at them. When you have a plan, you can start moving and proactively adjust your path as you see the landscape better.

Planning is a continual and rhythmic process, which you'll revise as life circumstances change, external environments shift or you learn something new. Be prepared to come back and review your plan every quarter (every three months) or as needed.

Above all, remember that even a bad plan is better than having no plan at all. It will help you become a victor of life, not a victim.

SET PRIORITIES

Successful people have laser-vision focus on their goals. They don't let shiny distractions—neither things nor people—detract them from their priorities.

If you do an inventory of your daily activities, you may be surprised to learn how much time you have mindlessly allocated to unimportant matters. Once you set your goals and design a plan, you must prioritize your time to do the work on that plan. This means reducing infatuations and addictions that don't match your vision or goals.

This doesn't mean letting go of fun things. Prioritize fun things as well as your work. What you need to get rid of are activities that don't align with your values or those time wasters that leave you feeling drained and worthless.

This may mean you need to stop watching reality television shows or reduce the hours you spend arguing with strangers on social media (who knows what I'm talking about?). You may need to decline those martini nights after work where all everyone does is complain about your dreadful bosses.

We all have bad habits. Let's shed them now we've got bigger plans on our plates.

There's a saying that *when you do the things today that others won't do, you'll have the things tomorrow that others will never have.* The small sacrifices you make today will bring you bigger and juicier rewards tomorrow.

It's a choice you'll have to make.

At the end of the day, you cannot blame anyone else for the results of the decisions you've made about your own life. So, make the right choices today.

PLAN YOUR WORK AND WORK YOUR PLAN

Everybody, including Richard Branson, Beyoncé, and Oprah, has the same twenty-four hours in their day just as we do. The question is, how will you use your twenty-four hours? That's what differentiates those who will be successful and those who will languish in mediocrity.

It was only recently that I redesigned my days to make sure I spend time on activities that bring me value. This meant using my calendar to book time for tasks on my action plans. I set reminders to alert me to when

I need to sit down and write. I curbed my social media habit and created daily rituals for the morning and evening to get the most important things done in the most efficient way possible.

Brendon Burchard, trainer and coach on high performance, says he only has to glance at someone's weekly schedule to predict how successful that person will become. It's not only what's in the calendars, but whether they are used. Do you use one? What does your calendar look like?

If you don't have one yet, go out and buy yourself a print calendar or sign up for any of the myriad of online schedules available. You don't have an excuse anymore. Schedule your work, set reminders, and stick to them.

STAY IN YOUR ZONE

One of the best decisions I made recently is to curb the time I interact with people who don't hold the same values as I do.

These people usually don't show much gratitude or passion for their lives. Most of them live like victims, meaning they let life happen to them rather than the other way around. I like to think they mean well but they have little self-awareness. They display negative tendencies like anger, apathy, and blame without even realizing it. They distract themselves with harmful addictions, love to gossip, get immersed in negative chitchat, and are in general unhappy inside.

The one common thread I saw through them all was how bitterly they carped about their lives but did nothing to make a change. If I ever queried about solutions or possibilities, they'd sit back with a defeatist shrug and say "What's the point?" Then, they'd immediately (and with disturbing enthusiasm) get right back to complaining.

It was hard to stay focused on my own dreams when I hung around them. I became unhappy too, complaining and not getting anywhere. Worst of all, I started to hate myself for it.

So little by little I cut out those coffee chats and supper outings. It wasn't easy to say no at first, but my peace of mind increased exponentially, and my level of stress decreased drastically once they transitioned out of my life.

This meant I found space to invite new people into my life, people with principles and good cheer. They encourage me to follow my dreams and give me the time, space, and support to focus on my own plans. They want to make a positive difference in their lives and those around them.

This idea may sound harsh and you may need time to apply it, but you must remove yourself from environments that harm you—inadvertently or otherwise. Prioritize the times you spend in your preferred zone. Your mental and physical health will improve and your sense of joy will increase the more you stay in your happy zone. I can promise you that.

None of this means you must lead a Grinch-like existence where you've got no friends and are manically working on one thing.

What this means is being mindful of how you spend your days and with whom. It means prioritizing what's most important to you and not what others tell you to. It also means learning to say no to people or opportunities or activities counterproductive to your health, well-being, or goals. And it means you may have to sacrifice a few things to realize your vision. Nothing gets done with magic.

REWARD YOURSELF

There is one more thing you can do to sweeten the deal.

Every time you hit a milestone in your plans, however big or small, give yourself a break or a small gift. This could be as simple as watching that show you love, eating your favorite treat, having a night out, or going on a date.

Whenever I finish a small milestone, I treat myself with a trip to one of my favorite exotic restaurants in town and feast on food I usually don't make at home. This entrenches the concept of **goal-plan-action-reward** in my mind and gets me enthusiastic about continuing on to the next stage of my plan. It's a small and affordable perk, and it works wonders.

When I hit larger goals like finishing an entire book, I give myself a bigger prize like a day hike in a park or a trip on a tour boat around the bay where I live, taking my camera with me. Just being out in nature re-energizes me, and I come back feeling like I truly deserved that amazing adventure. And then, I'm ready for the next phase of my work.

I know some women who treat themselves to a weekend at a spa and others who take their family to Disneyland to celebrate large goals. I also have friends who'll take a weekend off and watch their favorite show with a bucket of ice cream on their laps to reward themselves at the end of a large milestone.

Do whatever works for you, but don't forget to get off that couch and get back to your plans on Monday morning.

Giving yourself a bounty like this is a wonderful way to maintain momentum toward your vision and enjoy life while you're at it.

BE OPEN

While we all need a plan to guide us, our life journey should never be rigid. If it is, we may end up missing out on opportunities that may take us toward our vision even faster, or perhaps to more amazing adventures we can't conceive of today.

Your fundamental values will guide you and your plans will steer you. But always stay alert to new terrains. Be adaptable to changing environments that may require a detour. It's in those bends in the road of life that you come across life's most interesting and memorable moments.

We have to remain steadfast in our vision but be flexible in our plan on how we get to it.

Your Rebel Plans

"When I dare to be powerful, to use my strength in the service of my vision, then it becomes less important whether I am afraid."
Audre Lorde

ACTION PLANS

Okay, so how do we create plans for each of our SMART goals then? Take each of your goals, and ask yourself this question: What are the main action steps I need to take to achieve this goal?

If your goals meet the SMART criteria, you shouldn't have a problem coming up with appropriate plans. They should flow seamlessly and you should be able to think of a handful of logical steps you need to take next.

One to four actions per goal are generally sufficient. You don't want to overwhelm yourself with too many things to do. You also don't want to create such a tight schedule that you have no wiggle room. This will make it difficult for you to pivot if things change during the year.

Just remember to keep things as simple as possible and not overthink. We're not here to overcomplicate our lives. You're trying to create, as much as possible, an easy-to-follow map that will guide you to your dreams.

BE REASONABLY SPECIFIC

From all the components of the passion pyramid, these individual action plans are where you need to be the most specific. This is where you need to think of as many details as needed to complete the task at hand.

- Think of *how* you'll take action or the steps related to each activity.
- Decide on *when* you'll do these actions and *how long* they'll take.

🌿 Ask if any of these activities will *cost* you money, so you can budget for it.

🌿 Figure out *where* the action will take place so you can consider time, costs, and other requirements for travel or commuting if needed.

🌿 Think of *who* you'll partner with, or which of your mentors, colleagues, or friends will help you or join you in this action.

🌿 Brainstorm the highlights or expected results of your activities, so you have *milestones* to check progress against.

EXAMPLE

Here's an example of an action plan using Alice's SMART Goal #1.

Goals, just like plans, can vary in length and complexity. Alice's first goal is all about finding a "day job" to pay for rent and living expenses while she investigates her longer-range aim of a teaching career. This goal may not need three to six months depending on how hard she works and what the job market is like.

The milestones on this table help Alice check how well she's doing on her plan. We'll talk about measuring and tracking goals more in the next section, but if all you do is itemize the high-level results you expect to achieve by completing each action, you can easily track your work and see where you're losing or gaining ground.

If one of your goals is to look for a job as well, use this table as a template. Make sure to tailor it to your needs. The key thing to keep in mind is to match your plans to your goals and remain agile.

A plan like this will help you remember your most important tasks. It will help you to avoid wasting time or floundering unsure of what to do next.

SMART Goal #1: Move in with my parents and find a full-time job that will pay for our living expenses and allow me to pay off the lawyer fees in two years or less.	
Example Action #1	
WHAT will I do?	Plan
HOW will I make this happen?	Create a job search timeline & schedule activities in calendar. Calculate income needed for living expenses plus lawyer's fees. Do skills, knowledge & experience inventory & find out the jobs I'm qualified for. Update CV & create cover letter template to tailor later. Make business cards. Anticipate interview questions & write down answers.
HOW LONG will this action take?	1 week full-time
WHEN do I want it done by?	Set appropriate date
What's this going to COST?	Printing costs for business cards and CVs–if required
WHERE do I take this action?	Home, local library, local service groups
WHO do I need to work with?	Career counselors at social services offices–if available
What are my MILESTONES?	CV, cover letter template, business cards, job search plan with goals and timelines, potential interview Q&A list all completed.
Example Action #2	
WHAT will I do?	Research

HOW will I make this happen?	Research companies & contacts within commuting distance. Get names & numbers of employment agencies & networking groups relevant to me. Make a list of online job search sites. Study industry standards like salary ranges, work hours & type of work and culture. Organize & save research in spreadsheet or document for easy referencing. Research & prep for salary negotiations & practice.
HOW LONG will this action take?	1-2 weeks full-time
WHEN do I want it done by?	Set appropriate date
What's this going to COST?	No costs other than Internet time
WHERE do I take this action?	Home, local library, local service groups
WHO do I need to work with?	Career counselors at social services offices–if available
What are my MILESTONES?	Research completed & documented. Salary negotiations researched and practiced.

Example Action #3

WHAT will I do?	Outreach
HOW will I make this happen?	Contact former managers for references. Register with employment agencies & ask for meetings. Cold call company contacts & ask for information meetings. Attend relevant networking functions. Invite contacts for coffee chats & ask everyone for job leads. Keep log of all contacts. Follow up with every lead.
HOW LONG will this action take?	4-12 weeks full-time

WHEN do I want it done by?	Set appropriate date
What's this going to COST?	Bus tickets / passes or gas and parking for travel. Phone / call charges. Coffee/tea.
WHERE do I take this action?	Events, employment agency offices, company offices
WHO do I need to work with?	Former managers, employment agencies, company hiring managers
What are my MILESTONES?	Spoken with 5-10 relevant contacts every day through telephone, email, social media, or personally, and followed up on previous week's contacts

Example Action #4

WHAT will I do?	Apply
HOW will I make this happen?	Scour online job boards, newspapers & journals for jobs every day and apply for relevant & suitable advertised jobs. Send out personalized cover letters, CVs, applications or emails, asking for interviews. Research companies and industry & prepare for interviews. Get to interviews on time, and send thank you card or note afterward. Log all applications, interviews & responses. Follow up with every lead.
HOW LONG will this action take?	4-12 weeks full-time
WHEN do I want it done by?	Set appropriate date
What's this going to COST?	Bus tickets / passes or gas and parking for travel. Phone / call charges. Dry cleaning professional clothes.
WHERE do I take this action?	Company offices

WHO do I need to work with?	Employment agencies, company hiring managers, human resources managers or departments
What are my MILESTONES?	Applied for at least 5 jobs a day and followed up on previous week's contacts. Received callbacks from at least 10% of applied jobs.

Once you create a plan like this, the rest is easy.

You'll have to refer to it every few months and tick off what got done. But there's no need to go to the nth degree here.

You're not creating a plan for a multi-million-dollar program that will be analyzed to death by a bunch of priggish bureaucrats (yes, I worked in that field for way too long). All you need to do is get a good idea of what you must do next and how, when, where, and with whom, so you're prepared to proceed intelligently and well-informed.

Create the best plan you can to guide your next steps with the information you have now, then start moving. You can always adjust the plan later on as or if needed. You should be in action mode 95 percent of your time.

Never, ever get lost in perfection, for that will surely kill your vision.

> *"Life is not a dress rehearsal. Stop practicing what you're going to do and just do it. In one bold stroke you can transform today."*
> *Marilyn Grey*

Are you ready to move on to your action plans now?

In the next table, jot down in bullet form the main thoughts that jump into your mind under each column.

The biggest mistake you can make here is to get stuck in analysis paralysis. Stop immediately if you keep writing, crossing things out and writing again. Take a break, talk to a friend, or go for a walk. Clear your mind and come back when you're refreshed.

A few bullets per column is all you need. You don't need to create four actions because space is provided here. Find the most relevant activities to your personal goals. Maybe all you need is <u>one</u> profound action. And that's perfectly okay.

MY ACTION PLANS - QUESTION 1

SMART Goal #1:	
Action #1	
WHAT will I do?	
HOW will I make this happen?	
HOW LONG will this action take?	
WHEN do I want it done by?	
What's this going to **COST**?	
WHERE do I take this action?	
WHO do I need to work with?	
What are my **MILESTONES**?	

Your Rebel Plans

Action #2	
WHAT will I do?	
HOW will I make this happen?	
HOW LONG will this action take?	
WHEN do I want it done by?	
What's this going to COST?	
WHERE do I take this action?	
WHO do I need to work with?	
What are my MILESTONES?	
Action #3	
WHAT will I do?	
HOW will I make this happen?	
HOW LONG will this action take?	
WHEN do I want it done by?	
What's this going to COST?	
WHERE do I take this action?	
WHO do I need to work with?	
What are my MILESTONES?	

Action #4	
WHAT will I do?	
HOW will I make this happen?	
HOW LONG will this action take?	
WHEN do I want it done by?	
What's this going to COST?	
WHERE do I take this action?	
WHO do I need to work with?	
What are my MILESTONES?	

Your Rebel Plans

"Do you really want to look back on your life and see how wonderful it could have been had you not been afraid to live it?"
Caroline Myss

MY ACTION PLANS - QUESTION 2

SMART Goal #2:	
Action #1	
WHAT will I do?	
HOW will I make this happen?	
HOW LONG will this action take?	
WHEN do I want it done by?	
What's this going to COST?	
WHERE do I take this action?	
WHO do I need to work with?	
What are my MILESTONES?	

Action #2	
WHAT will I do?	
HOW will I make this happen?	
HOW LONG will this action take?	
WHEN do I want it done by?	
What's this going to COST?	
WHERE do I take this action?	
WHO do I need to work with?	
What are my MILESTONES?	
Action #3	
WHAT will I do?	
HOW will I make this happen?	
HOW LONG will this action take?	
WHEN do I want it done by?	
What's this going to COST?	
WHERE do I take this action?	
WHO do I need to work with?	
What are my MILESTONES?	

Action #4	
WHAT will I do?	
HOW will I make this happen?	
HOW LONG will this action take?	
WHEN do I want it done by?	
What's this going to COST?	
WHERE do I take this action?	
WHO do I need to work with?	
What are my MILESTONES?	

Your Rebel Plans

"The big secret in life is that there is no big secret. Whatever your goal, you can get there if you're willing to work."
Oprah Winfrey

MY ACTION PLANS - QUESTION 3

SMART Goal #3:	
Action #1	
WHAT will I do?	
HOW will I make this happen?	
HOW LONG will this action take?	
WHEN do I want it done by?	
What's this going to COST?	
WHERE do I take this action?	
WHO do I need to work with?	
What are my MILESTONES?	

Action #2

WHAT will I do?	
HOW will I make this happen?	
HOW LONG will this action take?	
WHEN do I want it done by?	
What's this going to COST?	
WHERE do I take this action?	
WHO do I need to work with?	
What are my MILESTONES?	

Action #3

WHAT will I do?	
HOW will I make this happen?	
HOW LONG will this action take?	
WHEN do I want it done by?	
What's this going to COST?	
WHERE do I take this action?	
WHO do I need to work with?	
What are my MILESTONES?	

Action #4	
WHAT will I do?	
HOW will I make this happen?	
HOW LONG will this action take?	
WHEN do I want it done by?	
What's this going to COST?	
WHERE do I take this action?	
WHO do I need to work with?	
What are my MILESTONES?	

Your Rebel Plans

"Some dream of worthy accomplishments, while others stay awake and do them."
Unknown

MY ACTION PLANS - QUESTION 4

SMART Goal #4:	
Action #1	
WHAT will I do?	
HOW will I make this happen?	
HOW LONG will this action take?	
WHEN do I want it done by?	
What's this going to COST?	
WHERE do I take this action?	
WHO do I need to work with?	
What are my MILESTONES?	

Your Rebel Plans

Action #2	
WHAT will I do?	
HOW will I make this happen?	
HOW LONG will this action take?	
WHEN do I want it done by?	
What's this going to COST?	
WHERE do I take this action?	
WHO do I need to work with?	
What are my MILESTONES?	
Action #3	
WHAT will I do?	
HOW will I make this happen?	
HOW LONG will this action take?	
WHEN do I want it done by?	
What's this going to COST?	
WHERE do I take this action?	
WHO do I need to work with?	
What are my MILESTONES?	

Action #4	
WHAT will I do?	
HOW will I make this happen?	
HOW LONG will this action take?	
WHEN do I want it done by?	
What's this going to COST?	
WHERE do I take this action?	
WHO do I need to work with?	
What are my MILESTONES?	

Your Rebel Plans

"The difference between successful people and others is how long they spend time feeling sorry for themselves."
Barbara Corcoran

MY ACTION PLANS – QUESTION 5
COMPLETE ONLY AS NECESSARY

SMART Goal #5:	
Action #1	
WHAT will I do?	
HOW will I make this happen?	
HOW LONG will this action take?	
WHEN do I want it done by?	
What's this going to COST?	
WHERE do I take this action?	
WHO do I need to work with?	
What are my MILESTONES?	

Your Rebel Plans

Action #2	
WHAT will I do?	
HOW will I make this happen?	
HOW LONG will this action take?	
WHEN do I want it done by?	
What's this going to COST?	
WHERE do I take this action?	
WHO do I need to work with?	
What are my MILESTONES?	
Action #3	
WHAT will I do?	
HOW will I make this happen?	
HOW LONG will this action take?	
WHEN do I want it done by?	
What's this going to COST?	
WHERE do I take this action?	
WHO do I need to work with?	
What are my MILESTONES?	

Action #4	
WHAT will I do?	
HOW will I make this happen?	
HOW LONG will this action take?	
WHEN do I want it done by?	
What's this going to COST?	
WHERE do I take this action?	
WHO do I need to work with?	
What are my MILESTONES?	

Your Rebel Plans

"Dear optimist, pessimist, and realist: While you guys were busy arguing about the glass of wine, I drank it! Sincerely, the opportunist!"
Lori Greiner

PUTTING IT ALL TOGETHER

Here's how the action plans, goals, and vision fit together in a goal map.

You can print this page and scribble on the image, or you can just write it all down on a piece of blank paper or whiteboard—whatever works best for you. Write everything in bullet form. We're not trying to draft an essay here, but create an easy-to-read plan we can refer to and put check marks against.

I like to have my vision, goals, and plans summarized on one sheet of paper. I pin this up at my home office so when I see it every day, it reminds me where my focus needs to be.

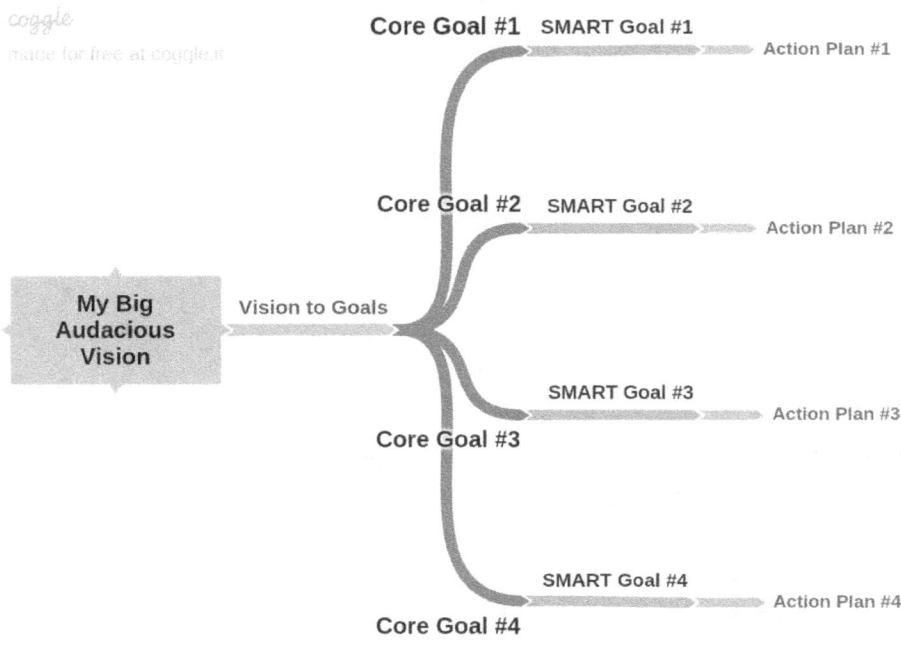

TRACK YOUR PLAN

You didn't do all this good work to shove this plan into a drawer or pin it somewhere and forget about it, did you? I regularly check my progress against milestones to see where I'm at. If you'd like a more detailed measurement method to help you stay organized, the next section will show you how.

SO, HOW DO YOU FEEL?

That's the end of this section. Write down anything you didn't capture in the questions but that you want to get out of your system.

1. How do you feel after completing this section?

- ○ Meh. Nothing interesting here
- ○ I really want to get this, but I'm lost and need help
- ○ I'm doing well. Just need to think some more
- ○ Fantastic. I've nailed this round. Woo-hoo!
- ○ Other: _____

2. What do you still need to figure out?

A.

B.

C.

3. What actions will you take in the next seven days to keep this topic on the top of your mind and clarify it further?

A.

B.

C.

BREAK

Fantastic work!

How did you find this section? Don't worry if you're exhausted. That only means your brain's been clicking away doing some awesome thinking.

If you've come this far, you now have a vision, a set of SMART goals, and your execution plan all done. That's amazing. You're part of a teensy tiny minority of people who don't just have big dreams but also have a structured, well-thought-out plan to get to them. You're now all set to embark on your new life adventure!

This is a good time to take a break and let all this marinate in your brain while you go about doing other things. Come back next week to move on to the next stage.

Enjoy your break. See you next week.

Tikiri

Your Rebel Plans

WEEK THREE

SECTION THREE CHECK-INS

How do I know I'm on track?

Success is most often achieved by those who don't know that failure is inevitable.

Coco Chanel

"So often people are working hard at the wrong thing. Working on the right thing is probably more important than working hard."
Caterina Fake

CHECKING IN ON OUR ACTIONS

Just like you need to keep an eye out for signposts and landmarks when you're climbing a mountain, you need to track your plans regularly to make sure you haven't veered off course.

By remaining vigilant, you'll quickly recognize dead ends or places you shouldn't be in before it's too late. You'll know when a plan of action is no longer working and it's time to cut your losses, turn around and find a better route to the top.

Doing a routine checkup on your status will also give you the time and space to apply new ideas that might pop up, ones that can give you greater dividends than your existing plans.

KEEP IT LOGICAL

So, how do you know you're on track on your execution plan?

To answer this question, you need to set a few solid milestones that will gauge how well you're progressing. These milestones shouldn't be complicated. They shouldn't be.

In Alice's SMART Goal #1 example, she merely created a list of tangible outcomes she expected to result from her actions. These included getting her CV done, business cards printed and speaking to a specific number of relevant contacts about jobs.

The milestones you select will depend on your action plan but remember to always keep them simple, easy to understand and easy to review.

Above all, make sure the milestones you choose are directly linked to the action you're performing. Otherwise, you'll be measuring the wrong thing which can take you off your path, away from your goals and even cost you in time and money.

Many large companies make this mistake. Where people or organizations go astray is when they start searching for "vanity metrics." These are milestones which make you feel good and may superficially look great, but have little to do with your progress.

Under Alice's Goal #1, she's tracking the number of people she speaks with about her job search. Should she count *all* the people she talks to including cousin Vinny, the celebrity dog trainer in Argentina and Jake, the long-time high-school friend who now runs an uber-wealth management firm in New York?

It's tempting to make your progress look good, but this can skew your assessment. While both Vinny and Jake are, I'm sure, fine folk, they may not be able to or have the time to help her reach her objective as a local teacher.

Alice needs to count the times she speaks to the *right* people in her field of interest. These are people who can assist her with relevant information and relevant leads to get her to her goal.

This is the time to engage that left brain of yours and get a little anal retentive (if you don't mind the term). Come up with relevant milestones for each plan by asking, "How will I know when this plan is done?" or "How will I know this action I'm about to do is successful?"

Create one milestone per action so you won't overwhelm yourself with data. Remember, you must make the time to review this information throughout the year.

Keep it logical. Keep it simple.

TIMING

How often should you review your plans?

This will depend on the size and complexity of your goals, but taking stock every one to three months is reasonable.

Pick a date each quarter (that's only four times a year) if that suits you and set aside thirty minutes to look over your plans. When the time comes, make yourself a cup of tea and see how well you're going. This is also a good time to ask yourself if your plans and even your goals are still valid given new circumstances or lessons you've learned over the past few months.

You may find all you need is to continue as planned. Or, you may find a goal needs adjusting, a plan needs to be removed or an action needs to be added.

Take your time as you go through this and remember you'll be doing this only four times annually. Two hours every year to see if your life's on track is worth it.

TOOLS TO USE

You don't need complicated systems to track your execution plan. It can be as simple as a tick mark next to each of your milestones on your action plan.

If, however, your actions are substantial and more long-term in nature, you can use the quarterly assessment tool shown on the upcoming pages to check your execution plan at fixed periods throughout the year.

TO SWITCH OR TO QUIT

One more thing before we look at the quarterly assessment tool.

How do you know when you've hit a dead end?

Sometimes, these are easy to identify, but most times you might see a small roadblock and think it's game over when it's really not.

Knowing when to turn back or stay on course requires a combination of astuteness and experience. The best way to tackle difficult problems is to stay as objective as possible by checking up on your milestones systematically and keeping your vision on top of your mind. This way, you don't let that ancient lizard brain of yours revert to flight or fight mode at a hint of problems.

Take the time to assess the situation, ask yourself if you're making the right assumptions and pull in a friend to brainstorm solutions if you need.

Sometimes roadblocks aren't true roadblocks. You may be able to easily slip around it, jump over it, crash through it, or even build a hoverboard and fly over it. You always have options. Always.

Now, let's consider the other side of this coin.

GETTING UNSTUCK

Some people make the mistake of sticking with the wrong plan for far too long. They continue even after they realize their milestones aren't being met consistently. Those roadblocks are now flashing neon red lights that scream, *Stop what you're doing!*

How many of you know what I'm talking about? We see this in our friends who remain in relationships that no longer work or in ourselves when we stay in jobs we no longer enjoy. Some of us continue on these miserable paths for years. I know what that's like—I got stuck in a job I hated for fifteen years before I made a move. Fifteen years!

We stay stuck because we're too afraid to break free, too anxious about change. When this happens, the best advice I can give you is to listen to your gut and take its advice seriously.

Every time I've hit a legitimate dead end, my stomach has sent red flag after red flag to warn me. It starts off with an uneasy feeling that something is off and moves on to full-blown tummy aches. In my early years, I ignored these signs to my detriment. Many mistakes later, I've learned to trust my instincts.

This doesn't mean I don't look at the issue objectively or think critically. I do both. I ask questions and check my criteria, but then, I also listen to my gut, especially when I know it's yelling at me to stop doing what I'm doing.

And remember, if you make a mistake, you can always turn back. Life's a big experiment where we try, learn, grow, and keep moving. Never punish yourself for hanging on to the wrong plan for too long or for choosing a plan that doesn't work. As soon as you correct course, forget about it and keep advancing on your new path.

Always look forward, not backward, because you're not going that way.

CELEBRATE

Don't forget what we said earlier about celebrating successes.

Putting a check mark next to a successfully achieved milestone will make you feel great. But why not savor that moment and let it really sink in with a small (or big) reward for yourself? That will become an incentive to continue on the journey toward your big audacious vision.

Okay, onto the tracking tool next.

Your Rebel Plans

> *"I've come to believe that each of us has a personal calling that's as unique as a fingerprint – and that the best way to succeed is to discover what you love and then find a way to offer it to others in the form of service, working hard, and also allowing the energy of the universe to lead you."*
> Oprah Winfrey

CHECK-IN ON MY ACTION PLANS – QUESTION 1

Let's move on to tracking your action plans now. Use this if you need a more thorough tracking mechanism for your action plans.

In the tables below, jot down in bullet form the key milestones per action. Then check back regularly to see how you're progressing.

These tables are delineated into quarters or three months per year. But choose the most suitable periods to review your plans. Maybe all you need is to check every six months.

The most important thing is to check your plans systematically but there's no need to go all-out crazy with it.

SMART Goal #1:

Your Rebel Plans

❏ **Quarter 1 Check:** _____ (e.g. January - March)

Action	Milestones	Was action completed?	COMPLETED ACTIONS		INCOMPLETE ACTIONS	
			Were milestones met?	If not, what went wrong and how will I improve next time?	Is action on track?	If not, what do I need to get it back on track?
Action #1		❏ Yes ❏ No	❏ Yes ❏ No		❏ Yes ❏ No	
Action #2		❏ Yes ❏ No	❏ Yes ❏ No		❏ Yes ❏ No	
Action #3		❏ Yes ❏ No	❏ Yes ❏ No		❏ Yes ❏ No	
Action #4		❏ Yes ❏ No	❏ Yes ❏ No		❏ Yes ❏ No	

❏ **Quarter 2 Check:** _____ (e.g. April - June)

Action	Milestones	Was action completed?	COMPLETED ACTIONS		INCOMPLETE ACTIONS	
			Were milestones met?	If not, what went wrong and how will I improve next time?	Is action on track?	If not, what do I need to get it back on track?
Action #1		❏ Yes ❏ No	❏ Yes ❏ No		❏ Yes ❏ No	
Action #2		❏ Yes ❏ No	❏ Yes ❏ No		❏ Yes ❏ No	
Action #3		❏ Yes ❏ No	❏ Yes ❏ No		❏ Yes ❏ No	
Action #4		❏ Yes ❏ No	❏ Yes ❏ No		❏ Yes ❏ No	

Your Rebel Plans

❏ **Quarter 3 Check:** _____ (e.g. July - September)

Action	Milestones	Was action completed?	COMPLETED ACTIONS		INCOMPLETE ACTIONS	
			Were milestones met?	If not, what went wrong and how will I improve next time?	Is action on track?	If not, what do I need to get it back on track?
Action #1		❏ Yes ❏ No	❏ Yes ❏ No		❏ Yes ❏ No	
Action #2		❏ Yes ❏ No	❏ Yes ❏ No		❏ Yes ❏ No	
Action #3		❏ Yes ❏ No	❏ Yes ❏ No		❏ Yes ❏ No	
Action #4		❏ Yes ❏ No	❏ Yes ❏ No		❏ Yes ❏ No	

❏ **Quarter 4 Check:** _____ (e.g. October - December)

Action	Milestones	Was action completed?	COMPLETED ACTIONS		INCOMPLETE ACTIONS	
			Were milestones met?	If not, what went wrong and how will I improve next time?	Is action on track?	If not, what do I need to get it back on track?
Action #1		❏ Yes ❏ No	❏ Yes ❏ No		❏ Yes ❏ No	
Action #2		❏ Yes ❏ No	❏ Yes ❏ No		❏ Yes ❏ No	
Action #3		❏ Yes ❏ No	❏ Yes ❏ No		❏ Yes ❏ No	
Action #4		❏ Yes ❏ No	❏ Yes ❏ No		❏ Yes ❏ No	

Your Rebel Plans

"Life-fulfilling work is never about the money -- when you feel true passion for something, you instinctively find ways to nurture it."
Eileen Fisher

CHECK-IN ON MY ACTION PLANS - QUESTION 2

SMART Goal #2:

Your Rebel Plans

❑ **Quarter 1 Check:** _____ (e.g. January - March)

Action	Milestones	Was action completed?	COMPLETED ACTIONS		INCOMPLETE ACTIONS	
			Were milestones met?	If not, what went wrong and how will I improve next time?	Is action on track?	If not, what do I need to get it back on track?
Action #1		❑ Yes ❑ No	❑ Yes ❑ No		❑ Yes ❑ No	
Action #2		❑ Yes ❑ No	❑ Yes ❑ No		❑ Yes ❑ No	
Action #3		❑ Yes ❑ No	❑ Yes ❑ No		❑ Yes ❑ No	
Action #4		❑ Yes ❑ No	❑ Yes ❑ No		❑ Yes ❑ No	

Tikiri

❏ **Quarter 2 Check:** _____ (e.g. April - June)

			COMPLETED ACTIONS		INCOMPLETE ACTIONS	
Action	Milestones	Was action completed?	Were milestones met?	If not, what went wrong and how will I improve next time?	Is action on track?	If not, what do I need to get it back on track?
Action #1		❏ Yes ❏ No	❏ Yes ❏ No		❏ Yes ❏ No	
Action #2		❏ Yes ❏ No	❏ Yes ❏ No		❏ Yes ❏ No	
Action #3		❏ Yes ❏ No	❏ Yes ❏ No		❏ Yes ❏ No	
Action #4		❏ Yes ❏ No	❏ Yes ❏ No		❏ Yes ❏ No	

Your Rebel Plans

❏ **Quarter 3 Check:** _____ (e.g. July - September)

Action	Milestones	Was action completed?	COMPLETED ACTIONS		INCOMPLETE ACTIONS	
			Were milestones met?	If not, what went wrong and how will I improve next time?	Is action on track?	If not, what do I need to get it back on track?
Action #1		❏ Yes ❏ No	❏ Yes ❏ No		❏ Yes ❏ No	
Action #2		❏ Yes ❏ No	❏ Yes ❏ No		❏ Yes ❏ No	
Action #3		❏ Yes ❏ No	❏ Yes ❏ No		❏ Yes ❏ No	
Action #4		❏ Yes ❏ No	❏ Yes ❏ No		❏ Yes ❏ No	

❏ **Quarter 4 Check:** _____ (e.g. October - December)

Action	Milestones	Was action completed?	COMPLETED ACTIONS		INCOMPLETE ACTIONS	
			Were milestones met?	If not, what went wrong and how will I improve next time?	Is action on track?	If not, what do I need to get it back on track?
Action #1		❏ Yes ❏ No	❏ Yes ❏ No		❏ Yes ❏ No	
Action #2		❏ Yes ❏ No	❏ Yes ❏ No		❏ Yes ❏ No	
Action #3		❏ Yes ❏ No	❏ Yes ❏ No		❏ Yes ❏ No	
Action #4		❏ Yes ❏ No	❏ Yes ❏ No		❏ Yes ❏ No	

Your Rebel Plans

"You may be disappointed if you fail, but you are doomed if you don't try."
Beverly Sills

CHECK-IN ON MY ACTION PLANS – QUESTION 3

SMART Goal #3:

Your Rebel Plans

❏ **Quarter 1 Check:** _____ (e.g. January - March)

Action	Milestones	Was action completed?	COMPLETED ACTIONS		INCOMPLETE ACTIONS	
			Were milestones met?	If not, what went wrong and how will I improve next time?	Is action on track?	If not, what do I need to get it back on track?
Action #1		❏ Yes ❏ No	❏ Yes ❏ No		❏ Yes ❏ No	
Action #2		❏ Yes ❏ No	❏ Yes ❏ No		❏ Yes ❏ No	
Action #3		❏ Yes ❏ No	❏ Yes ❏ No		❏ Yes ❏ No	
Action #4		❏ Yes ❏ No	❏ Yes ❏ No		❏ Yes ❏ No	

❑ **Quarter 2 Check:** _____ (e.g. April - June)

Action	Milestones	Was action completed?	COMPLETED ACTIONS		INCOMPLETE ACTIONS	
			Were milestones met?	If not, what went wrong and how will I improve next time?	Is action on track?	If not, what do I need to get it back on track?
Action #1		❑ Yes ❑ No	❑ Yes ❑ No		❑ Yes ❑ No	
Action #2		❑ Yes ❑ No	❑ Yes ❑ No		❑ Yes ❑ No	
Action #3		❑ Yes ❑ No	❑ Yes ❑ No		❑ Yes ❑ No	
Action #4		❑ Yes ❑ No	❑ Yes ❑ No		❑ Yes ❑ No	

Your Rebel Plans

❏ **Quarter 3 Check:** _____ (e.g. July - September)

Action	Milestones	Was action completed?	COMPLETED ACTIONS		INCOMPLETE ACTIONS	
			Were milestones met?	If not, what went wrong and how will I improve next time?	Is action on track?	If not, what do I need to get it back on track?
Action #1		❏ Yes ❏ No	❏ Yes ❏ No		❏ Yes ❏ No	
Action #2		❏ Yes ❏ No	❏ Yes ❏ No		❏ Yes ❏ No	
Action #3		❏ Yes ❏ No	❏ Yes ❏ No		❏ Yes ❏ No	
Action #4		❏ Yes ❏ No	❏ Yes ❏ No		❏ Yes ❏ No	

❏ **Quarter 4 Check:** _____ (e.g. October - December)

Action	Milestones	Was action completed?	COMPLETED ACTIONS		INCOMPLETE ACTIONS	
			Were milestones met?	If not, what went wrong and how will I improve next time?	Is action on track?	If not, what do I need to get it back on track?
Action #1		❏ Yes ❏ No	❏ Yes ❏ No		❏ Yes ❏ No	
Action #2		❏ Yes ❏ No	❏ Yes ❏ No		❏ Yes ❏ No	
Action #3		❏ Yes ❏ No	❏ Yes ❏ No		❏ Yes ❏ No	
Action #4		❏ Yes ❏ No	❏ Yes ❏ No		❏ Yes ❏ No	

Your Rebel Plans

"Find the smartest people you can and surround yourself with them."
Marissa Meyer

CHECK-IN ON MY ACTION PLANS - QUESTION 4

SMART Goal #4:

Your Rebel Plans

❏ **Quarter 1 Check:** _____ (e.g. January - March)

Action	Milestones	Was action completed?	COMPLETED ACTIONS		INCOMPLETE ACTIONS	
			Were milestones met?	If not, what went wrong and how will I improve next time?	Is action on track?	If not, what do I need to get it back on track?
Action #1		❏ Yes ❏ No	❏ Yes ❏ No		❏ Yes ❏ No	
Action #2		❏ Yes ❏ No	❏ Yes ❏ No		❏ Yes ❏ No	
Action #3		❏ Yes ❏ No	❏ Yes ❏ No		❏ Yes ❏ No	
Action #4		❏ Yes ❏ No	❏ Yes ❏ No		❏ Yes ❏ No	

❏ **Quarter 2 Check:** _____ (e.g. April - June)

Action	Milestones	Was action completed?	COMPLETED ACTIONS		INCOMPLETE ACTIONS	
			Were milestones met?	If not, what went wrong and how will I improve next time?	Is action on track?	If not, what do I need to get it back on track?
Action #1		❏ Yes ❏ No	❏ Yes ❏ No		❏ Yes ❏ No	
Action #2		❏ Yes ❏ No	❏ Yes ❏ No		❏ Yes ❏ No	
Action #3		❏ Yes ❏ No	❏ Yes ❏ No		❏ Yes ❏ No	
Action #4		❏ Yes ❏ No	❏ Yes ❏ No		❏ Yes ❏ No	

Your Rebel Plans

❏ **Quarter 3 Check:** _____ (e.g. July - September)

			COMPLETED ACTIONS		INCOMPLETE ACTIONS	
Action	Milestones	Was action completed?	Were milestones met?	If not, what went wrong and how will I improve next time?	Is action on track?	If not, what do I need to get it back on track?
Action #1		❏ Yes ❏ No	❏ Yes ❏ No		❏ Yes ❏ No	
Action #2		❏ Yes ❏ No	❏ Yes ❏ No		❏ Yes ❏ No	
Action #3		❏ Yes ❏ No	❏ Yes ❏ No		❏ Yes ❏ No	
Action #4		❏ Yes ❏ No	❏ Yes ❏ No		❏ Yes ❏ No	

❑ **Quarter 4 Check:** _____ (e.g. October - December)

Action	Milestones	Was action completed?	COMPLETED ACTIONS		INCOMPLETE ACTIONS	
			Were milestones met?	If not, what went wrong and how will I improve next time?	Is action on track?	If not, what do I need to get it back on track?
Action #1		❑ Yes ❑ No	❑ Yes ❑ No		❑ Yes ❑ No	
Action #2		❑ Yes ❑ No	❑ Yes ❑ No		❑ Yes ❑ No	
Action #3		❑ Yes ❑ No	❑ Yes ❑ No		❑ Yes ❑ No	
Action #4		❑ Yes ❑ No	❑ Yes ❑ No		❑ Yes ❑ No	

Your Rebel Plans

"One of the most courageous things you can do is identify yourself, know who you are, what you believe in and where you want to go."
Sheila Murray Bethel

CHECK-IN ON MY ACTION PLANS - QUESTION 5
COMPLETE ONLY AS NECESSARY

SMART Goal 5:

Your Rebel Plans

❏ **Quarter 1 Check:** _____ (e.g. January - March)

Action	Milestones	Was action completed?	COMPLETED ACTIONS		INCOMPLETE ACTIONS	
			Were milestones met?	If not, what went wrong and how will I improve next time?	Is action on track?	If not, what do I need to get it back on track?
Action #1		❏ Yes ❏ No	❏ Yes ❏ No		❏ Yes ❏ No	
Action #2		❏ Yes ❏ No	❏ Yes ❏ No		❏ Yes ❏ No	
Action #3		❏ Yes ❏ No	❏ Yes ❏ No		❏ Yes ❏ No	
Action #4		❏ Yes ❏ No	❏ Yes ❏ No		❏ Yes ❏ No	

❏ **Quarter 2 Check:** _____ (e.g. April - June)

			COMPLETED ACTIONS		INCOMPLETE ACTIONS	
Action	Milestones	Was action completed?	Were milestones met?	If not, what went wrong and how will I improve next time?	Is action on track?	If not, what do I need to get it back on track?
Action #1		❏ Yes ❏ No	❏ Yes ❏ No		❏ Yes ❏ No	
Action #2		❏ Yes ❏ No	❏ Yes ❏ No		❏ Yes ❏ No	
Action #3		❏ Yes ❏ No	❏ Yes ❏ No		❏ Yes ❏ No	
Action #4		❏ Yes ❏ No	❏ Yes ❏ No		❏ Yes ❏ No	

Your Rebel Plans

❏ **Quarter 3 Check:** _____ (e.g. July - September)

Action	Milestones	Was action completed?	COMPLETED ACTIONS		INCOMPLETE ACTIONS	
			Were milestones met?	If not, what went wrong and how will I improve next time?	Is action on track?	If not, what do I need to get it back on track?
Action #1		❏ Yes ❏ No	❏ Yes ❏ No		❏ Yes ❏ No	
Action #2		❏ Yes ❏ No	❏ Yes ❏ No		❏ Yes ❏ No	
Action #3		❏ Yes ❏ No	❏ Yes ❏ No		❏ Yes ❏ No	
Action #4		❏ Yes ❏ No	❏ Yes ❏ No		❏ Yes ❏ No	

❑ **Quarter 4 Check:** _____ (e.g. October - December)

Action	Milestones	Was action completed?	COMPLETED ACTIONS		INCOMPLETE ACTIONS	
			Were milestones met?	If not, what went wrong and how will I improve next time?	Is action on track?	If not, what do I need to get it back on track?
Action #1		❑ Yes ❑ No	❑ Yes ❑ No		❑ Yes ❑ No	
Action #2		❑ Yes ❑ No	❑ Yes ❑ No		❑ Yes ❑ No	
Action #3		❑ Yes ❑ No	❑ Yes ❑ No		❑ Yes ❑ No	
Action #4		❑ Yes ❑ No	❑ Yes ❑ No		❑ Yes ❑ No	

Your Rebel Plans

"Our fear of the unknown and our fear of making mistakes trick us into focusing on what we don't know or can't do. When we give ourselves the freedom to be uncertain and less than perfect, then we can start thinking, 'What do I know? What can I do?' That's when the adventure starts—learning, thriving, conquering, failing, recouping, and having a ton of fun."
Kristin Smith

UNCERTAINTY

If there's one thing we can be certain of in life, it's uncertainty.

Nothing is guaranteed and no one has a crystal ball to predict the future.

What most people don't realize is that uncertainty is neutral. This means the future can hold either negative or positive potential. As women with a vision in life and the desire to move forward, we need to become comfortable with ambiguity. We need to learn to make decisions without having all the cards in our hands.

If we wait for the correct answers and the perfect plans before taking action, we'll remain stuck forever. And that is the greatest risk of them all.

When we don't make decisions out of fear of what the future might bring, we expose ourselves to whatever life throws our way. When we start moving forward, however, we can stay alert and change direction to avoid bumps and proactively move where we want to go.

This means the route to our dreams will not be a straight line but one with twists and turns along the way. It will be a squiggly line going up. This is something we need to accept and get comfortable with if we wish to succeed.

OBSTACLES

Obstacles are a fact of life and not always a sign that your vision or your goals aren't good enough.

The best way to prepare for problems that may crop up in your journey is to anticipate them in advance and think how to best address them.

When you're mentally ready for future risks and have a general idea of how you'll respond, you'll find yourself in a powerful position where few things unsettle you. You'll feel more balanced and ready to face the problems on your route, even those you haven't thought of yet.

If you ignore potential risks altogether, that could open you up to nasty surprises in the future. And if you're not prepared to face these obstacles, you may feel like quitting at the first sight of one.

Just remember, you cannot and should never forecast and prepare for all potential risks or you'll get immobilized with fear. The trick is to find a balance here.

TURNING THINGS AROUND

Even when we risk a negative outcome, things may not be as bad as we expect.

It's hard not to feel anxious when there's no certainty to the outcome. But many times, it's those experiences we're most apprehensive about which become our greatest allies. They can open our eyes to life lessons or exciting new opportunities we wouldn't have spotted otherwise.

This is another of those easier-said-than-done concepts, but if you look back at your own life, I'm sure you can think of instances where you grappled with uncertainty and turned obstacles into successes.

Let's make a list so you know how far you've come, and in turn, how much farther you're capable of going.

Write down those incidents in your life where you felt things were going to hell in a handbasket but that in fact helped you learn valuable lessons and turn your life around.

1. Life Event
What turned around:

2. Life Event
What turned around:

3. Life Event
What turned around:

Reread this list whenever you're having a difficult "one-of-those" days. Look at what you're capable of and gain strength from your own past.

SO, HOW DO YOU FEEL?

That's the end of this section. Write down anything you didn't capture in the questions but that you want to get out of your system.

1. How do you feel after completing this section?

- ○ Meh. Nothing interesting here
- ○ I really want to get this, but I'm lost and need help
- ○ I'm doing well. Just need to think some more
- ○ Fantastic. I've nailed this round. Woo-hoo!
- ○ Other: _____

2. What do you still need to figure out?

A.

B.

C.

3. What actions will you take in the next seven days to keep this topic on the top of your mind and clarify it further?

A.

B.

C.

WEEK FOUR

SECTION FOUR MY SCHEDULE

How do I optimize my time?

*I attribute my success to this:
I never gave or took any excuse.*

Florence Nightingale

"Excellence is an art won by training and habituation. We do not act rightly because we have virtue or excellence, but we rather have those because we have acted rightly. We are what we repeatedly do. Excellence, then, is not an act but a habit."
Aristotle

HOW TO GET THINGS DONE

I know what you're thinking. Jeez! *How in goodness' sake will I ever get all these* (insert your favorite cuss word here) *plans and check-ins done?*

So here's my question: how badly do you want your dream?

If you want it badly enough, you'll prioritize your time. I even have a few time-management tools in this section to help you here.

But what about those really bad days? you may be asking.

There will be times when you won't feel the motivation. You might have a setback or just one of those days when any interest on working on your goals fly out the window.

The best way to make sure you work on your plan every day is to adopt a series of good habits that will keep you on track regardless of your mood or negative external events. These habits will keep your spirits up and create the right environment and mindset so you'll stay on your game no matter what.

So, what are these habits?

Here are thirteen basic habits you can put to practice right away.

The word "habits" is an icky term that scares most people away but trust me, these are not that difficult to adapt and will make you feel better and become more productive in the long run.

Build them one by one and give yourself the time and space to incorporate them into your life. Don't give up until you've tried one idea for at least twenty days straight.

Are you ready?

1. Get good sleep. Your brain is the most important and powerful organ in your body. Take care of it and it will take care of you. You can do this by keeping it active by continuously learning new things and by also giving it the rejuvenation time it needs. This happens at night when you're sound asleep. This is when your brain goes into prep mode sorting all your thoughts and memories to get you rested and prepared for the next day. Don't deny your brain the time it needs to do this important job. Get your sleep.

2. Wake up early. If you can get up before the hustle and bustle of the day begins, you'll find the time and the space to get things done without distractions. Get up an hour earlier than usual, or even half an hour, and you'll find external interruptions are minimized if not eliminated. This is the best way to find time to get more done.

3. Exercise. Moving your body helps to energize your brain. Your mood will lift and you'll be in a better state, physically and mentally, to tackle your tasks of the day. Find at least ten minutes to workout before you sit down to work.

4. Protect your sacred time. Checking email or social media the minute you wake up is the best way to get pulled into distractions or mired in other peoples' dramas, demands, and agendas. The best thing you can do for yourself is to keep your phone on airplane mode after waking up, at least until you've taken time for yourself by exercising, meditating, reading or just being fully present with your family over a healthy breakfast. You'll find your mind will be clearer and your productivity will increase if you protect that sacred me-time first thing in the morning.

5. Get organized. Some of you won't like to hear this as you may be one of the rare people who can create magic among chaos. But for the rest of us, we need an uncluttered mind and an uncluttered space to get our work done efficiently. This reduces distractions and allows us to focus fully on the task at hand. So clean up your workspace. Organize your information, files, folders, tools, equipment, and email. Try it and see how much this will help you get things done faster.

6. Schedule it in. We all have good intentions and want to get things done, but unless we make the time to focus on that activity, it will rarely get done. Use a paper or online calendar and schedule your activities in it. Do this on a weekly or daily basis and you'll see your productivity increase exponentially.

7. Start small. If you went through all the exercises in this workbook you'll have seen that our main strategy has been to break things down to bite-sized chunks. Use this philosophy for everything you do. It's easy to set big goals, and it's just as easy to get overwhelmed and give up too soon. Everything can be broken into small steps. Find what the smallest task is and do that. As a writer, I tell myself I only have to write one good sentence every day, but of course, I don't stop there. I write another and another and by the end of the day have thousands of words down. Once you start with the teeniest activity, you'll invariably move on to the next one and the next until you've accomplished phenomenal work.

8. Make decisions faster. The best way to lose precious time and energy is to go over the same memos, letters, emails or notes again, and again, trying to decide what to do with them. I find the best strategy is to look at one thing once, decide and move on. You have four options here: get it done right away, delete it as it has no relevance to you, delegate it to someone else to do, or put it in a folder to action later. At the beginning, you'll be creating "to-do-later" folders all over the place but with time and practice, you'll learn to curtail this and make decisions more quickly. Most of the time, the first instinct you have will be the right one.

9. Apply the 80/20 rule. Pareto's Principle says 80 percent of your results come from 20 percent of your effort. We do many things during the day, but our progress will come from only 20 percent of those activities. Do an audit of your day (there's a tool in the next page for this), and ask yourself if your activities give you the most effective results or are they extraneous and useless? Do you do things because that's what you've always done, or because they get you closer to your goals? Take stock and adjust accordingly.

10. Measure your work. You've already done an entire exercise on how to track your main action plans. You can go further by tracking your daily activities. Keeping tab of the little things can motivate you to compete with yourself and finish that task you've been measuring. This is how I went from being a junk food omnivore to a healthy vegan. I noted the times I stuck to vegan meals and put this in my journal every night. Soon, I was pushing myself to go from 10 percent of vegan eating to 20 percent, then 50 percent and finally all the way to 100 percent. Measure your results however small they are, compete with yourself and have fun with it. It works wonders.

11. Batch process. When you have a series of tasks, look for ways to increase efficiency by doing them at the same time or sequencing them. If you're traveling to a certain place, can you think of all the other things you can do while you're there, so you don't have to make a second trip? If you're setting something up (for example cameras and lights to create a video), can you do several of the same tasks (create several videos) so you don't have to recreate that setup again? Create templates for anything you write more than once, so you don't have to reproduce the same framework every time.

12. Time your work. Have you heard of the Pomodoro Technique? It's a great time management method that breaks your work into short chunks of time. This simple tool can reduce distractions and enhance productivity. So, you will work for twenty-five minutes and take a break for five minutes. Every fourth break can be longer than the previous one and up to twenty minutes. I've adjusted this method slightly to meet my needs. I sit down and work for three-quarters of an hour and take five to ten-minute breaks when I get up, stretch, walk about, and fill up my mug of water. This way, I get recharged every hour and my focus increases. Also, knowing a timer will go off in forty-five minutes keeps my attention on the task. You can tailor this technique to best suit your needs.

13. Learn to say no. Everybody wants our time and attention. It's up to us to choose wisely what's most important to us and where our focus needs to be. Otherwise, we'll easily become a puppet in someone else's game. We need to take control of our priorities and respectfully decline invitations, calls, text messages, emails, events or any other activities that do not match our own goals and priorities. The mental energy we spend on people or activities that don't matter or don't interest us can drain us and even impact our self-esteem and confidence. It can also affect our productivity and progress. So, be careful to whom and for what you say yes.

Your Rebel Plans

> *"Because there is that sort of feeling that people don't know what to do with gaps in their lives. It's a scary notion, but actually, if you can stand in space just for a little while, a new door will open, or you'll be able to see in the dark after a while. You'll adjust."*
> Jane Campion

WHAT ARE YOU DOING RIGHT NOW?

You've done outstanding work.

You looked at your big audacious vision. You identified your core goals and translated them into SMART ones. You created an execution plan and know how you'll implement it over the course of the year. You've even come up with a system to track your progress.

Bravo!

So far, you've been focusing on the long-term. What we often forget, though, is how we spend this *current moment of time* may be the most important decision we make.

Our lives are made up of years which are comprised of months. Months contain weeks, and weeks contain days. Days, in turn, are made of hours, minutes, and seconds.

It's how we spend our seconds and minutes that count the most. It's the everyday small acts that will eventually lead us to our big audacious vision. Setting goals and plans helps us stay on track and get to our dreams faster but we need to always be paying attention to the now. What we choose to do in this moment determines whether we'll accomplish our plans, succeed in our goals, or achieve our vision.

Pause for a second (no pun intended) and take stock of how you spend the smallest denominator of time that makes sense to you. If you keep an account of these daily moments, I promise you, the findings will be eye-opening.

A SELF-AUDIT

Let's do that right now.

Here's a simple tool for you to record your hourly activities on any given day. Since each day of the week demands different routines and because weekends are usually not like weekdays, keep a tally of a full week from Monday to Sunday. You only have to do this once.

Doing this mini audit will show where you're spending your time and on what. You can then clean up your week and design your days to get you closer to your big audacious vision. This is how you can increase the most important activities (the 20 percent) that give you the most desirable (80 percent) results.

Once you complete this exercise, you'll have the right information to create your ideal day—which you'll do in the next exercise.

MY EXPERIENCE

When I did this exercise, I learned to my surprise that I dragged my feet for half an hour every morning before my physical workout. I was procrastinating, getting lost in social media, scrolling through depressing news headlines or mindlessly reading email.

These are all unhealthy activities to start the day with. They are a waste of time and usually leaves me feeling glum and idle for the rest of the day.

While I still have to kick myself (mentally) to get on my workout mat, just being aware of this one bad habit and how it affected my day has helped me to avoid it. Eliminate it.

The other important lesson I learned from this one week of record keeping is that when I know I'm watching and tracking myself, I'm more careful of what I do throughout the day. This exercise was a wake-up call for me to become more mindful of how I spend my time. It was also a call to action to spend my days on activities and people that bring me value and joy.

Your turn now.

How are you spending your hours and days?

Time of Day	What I Find Myself Doing During This Hour						
	Mon	**Tues**	**Wed**	**Thurs**	**Fri**	**Sat**	**Sun**
5:00–6:00am							
6:00–7:00am							
7:00–8:00am							
8:00–9:00am							
9:00–10:00am							
10:00–11:00am							
11:00–12:00pm							
12:00–1:00pm							

Your Rebel Plans

Time of Day	Mon	Tues	Wed	Thurs	Fri	Sat	Sun
1:00-2:00pm							
2:00-3:00pm							
3:00-4:00pm							
4:00-5:00pm							
5:00-6:00pm							
6:00-7:00pm							
7:00-8:00pm							
8:00-9:00pm							
9:00-10:00pm							
10:00-11:00pm							
11:00-12:00am							
12:00-5:00am							

"Seize every opportunity you have, embrace every experience. Make a mark for all the right reasons."
Chrissie Wellington

TWENTY-FOUR HOURS FOR ALL OF US

A majority of North America's billionaires (yes, that's with a "b") are self-made.

They didn't have large inheritances, important contacts, or limitless resources when they started out. What they had was a vision of some sort from which they set goals and created action plans. Then, they used their time every day (they have twenty-four hours just like we do) as wisely as they could.

The difference between them and those on the other end of the spectrum—barring exceptional circumstances—is what they focused on in the twenty-four hours they had.

It's what you focus on every day that makes a difference between you becoming successful in life or not.

You have a choice. You can spend your time on mindless and unproductive activities and focusing on what you don't have, complaining about it or blaming others about it. Or you can focus on what you can do right now to solve your problems, then put all your attention to it and give it your best every single day.

What you do every day says a lot about where you'll be tomorrow.

MY IDEAL DAY

Knowing this, what would your ideal day look like? How would you like to spend your days if you want to achieve your vision?

Use this scheduling table to jot down what you want to pay attention to at different times of the day. You don't need to break your days into every hour and every minute because that would stifle (and even paralyze) you, but identify what you want to pay attention to during your mornings, afternoons, and evenings at least.

When you do this, schedule things in at the times that work best for you.

For example, I slot my writing time into the mornings when my mind is most fresh and creative. I put all my marketing and client meetings in the afternoon and fun stuff like movies, drinks, and restaurant outings in the evenings when my brain has depleted its daily reserve.

I also add in preparation time. If I have to be somewhere for a business rendezvous, I add prep and travel time before the meeting and travel-back-home time plus a post-meeting review. This way, I'm always prepared, on time, and can quickly follow up on the discussion.

If I had to think about all these different things as I scurried along throughout the day, I'd never be on time, never follow up with the right people or have the required information lined up. I'd feel harried and drained by four. I know because that's exactly how it used to be.

This simple practice of scheduling my activities has led to huge improvements in my productivity and self-satisfaction compared to previous years when I struggled to get things done, which left me feeling frustrated.

The strange thing is when you plan your time and put structure into your days, you'll find more time for the fun stuff. Plus, you'll enjoy those times more. It's counterintuitive I know, but you'll be surprised how well this works.

SCHEDULE YOUR DAY

Once you figure out what your ideal day looks like, schedule it in a proper calendar—whether it's on a sheet of paper, a whiteboard on your wall, or in an electronic calendar. This is the best way to make sure work gets done.

I use an electronic calendar linked to my email so I can manage all my information in one place, including meeting requests that come to my inbox. You could try a few free and well-known apps like Google calendar, Outlook.com calendar, the Apple calendar, or any other scheduling software that comes with the messaging or email program you may already have on your phone or tablet.

Just keep in mind your schedule isn't written in blood. It shouldn't make you feel like you're chained down or you'll abandon the plan altogether soon enough. It's a frame of reference, albeit a powerful one, for you to organize your time.

Fill it with activities of your choosing and keep it flexible in case of emergencies or major interruptions. Give yourself free time periods to think, reflect, have fun and just be. Think of this as a framework within which you can live a stress-free life and still get your action plans done as you work toward your vision.

If you follow a schedule like this for one full month, you'll find it becomes a habit you don't even have to think about anymore. You'll reach for your calendar every day to plan and check. Things will get done—things you want to do, and you'll be on your way to living the life you desire.

MY EXPERIENCE

Once I wrote my plans down and scheduled them in my online calendar, I had to remind myself to check it only for the first couple of weeks. After that, using my schedule became an essential part of my day.

My daily priorities became ingrained in my mind and I instinctively knew what I had to focus on during that part of the day, and so went about doing it. When I made adjustments to my schedule, they came only from the actions plans I was tackling that month.

After a few months of using this tool, I settled into a routine, and surprisingly, it became a pleasant one.

Planning your time and sticking to it is only a chore when the work is not enjoyable or you're working to meet someone else's demands. When you fill your schedule with work you love—at this point that is what you must do—every day will become an ideal one.

Life is short and precious. It's up to us to make the right choices on how we spend our time, so why not make every day amazing?

So, what does your ideal day look like?

Time	Time of Day	What I'll Focus On:
5:00-6:00am	Morning	
6:00-7:00am		
7:00-8:00am		
8:00-9:00am		
9:00-10:00am		
10:00-11:00am		
11:00-12:00pm		

Time	Time of Day	What I'll Focus On:
12:00-1:00pm	Afternoon	
1:00-2:00pm		
2:00-3:00pm		
3:00-4:00pm		
4:00-5:00pm		
5:00-6:00pm		
6:00-7:00pm	Evening	
7:00-8:00pm		
8:00-9:00pm		
9:00-10:00pm		
10:00-11:00pm		

Your Rebel Plans

Time	Time of Day	What I'll Focus On:
11:00-12:00am	Evening	
12:00-1:00am		

"You may be disappointed if you fail, but you are doomed if you don't try."
Beverly Sills

MAKING LISTS

Here's a suggestion if you don't like to make a schedule. Plan a daily list of things to do the night before.

If you do this every evening, you'll go to bed feeling settled knowing you've got tomorrow covered, even if today hadn't gone as planned.

I used this practice successfully for years at my corporate job, even when there were many uncertainties and time was not mine most of the time. Despite that chaotic environment, I got things done with this simple, daily practice of creating a prioritized list the night before.

IMPORTANT VERSUS URGENT

So, how do we prioritize our lists?

In his legendary book, *The Seven Habits of Highly Effective People*, Stephen Covey explains the importance of differentiating between what's important and what's urgent on our lists. Just because something is flashing red in front of us doesn't make it a must-do-now item.

This is hard to apply at first because we're so used to jumping up for ringing tones, alarms, alerts, and myriads of mostly inconsequential noise that vie for our attention. Most times, we're the ones who've allowed these disruptions to permeate our lives. As Stephen Covey explains in his book, we must reduce trivial items (and people) from our lists and keep them from becoming urgent in the first place.

One thing we can do is turn off all the notifications coming from our electronic devices, at least until we're done with our highest priority work. Our daily goal should be to focus our attention on the work that will get us closer to our vision. We need to take care of the small things early on so they don't grow into giant crisis monsters that howl for our attention at the most inopportune times.

All the goal setting, action planning and risk busting we've learned so far are designed to reduce unwanted emergencies. We can never eliminate crisis situations, but we can get a clear indication of what a true emergency looks like compared to something that will suck our time but do nothing to move us forward.

So when you write down your list every night, put the most important items on top. Differentiate between what feels urgent but brings little value and what's important and will move you forward toward your goals. Try to reduce, delegate, or remove all those unimportant activities altogether from your life.

KISS THAT FROG

One of the biggest mistakes people make when they use daily lists is tackling the easiest items first.

I've been guilty of this many times.

Every night before bed, I'd make a long list of priorities for the next day. Then, in the morning, I'd spend my most creative and alert period on easy tasks because I could tackle them quickly and I wanted to tick them off. When I got to the more complex and difficult items later in the day, my brain had depleted and since I was not as attentive, my productivity plummeted.

Being busy didn't mean I was progressing on my action plans. I was procrastinating on my major goals and didn't even realize it.

It took herculean effort to make the switch. One trick that helped was to write down only the most difficult high-priority task for the next day—a task that came directly from my execution plan and one that, if done right, would solve many of the little problems and tasks as well. This was my one thing for the day.

This idea comes from the book *Eat That Frog*, based on an insightful quote from Mark Twain. He said, "If it's your job to eat a frog, it's best to do it first thing in the morning. And if it's your job to eat two frogs, it's best to eat the biggest one first." Being vegan, I'd rather say kiss the frog instead. Still icky to do, but much more compassionate.

So I put down the biggest "frog" on my list every night. Then I highlighted it and underlined it. I told myself if that was all I accomplished the next day, that would be enough. In fact, that would be awesome.

Every morning, I woke to my biggest frog staring me in the face. There were no distractions. There was nothing to debate. I had no choice but to kiss it. So I rolled up my sleeves and got to work.

The good news is I could still tackle the fast and easy items later in the day. Emails, meetings, phone calls, booking an oil change for my car, making an appointment with the dentist, or picking up groceries all fall into this category, as they don't require the same amount of focus and brainpower as my most creative work.

Remember that trick your teacher did at school? The one where they filled a jar with sand and then tried to ram a rock in it but it didn't fit? What did they do next? They took a new jar, put the big rock in first and then poured the sand in to show how you need to get the big things done first. Take care of those big rocks (or the big frog) first, and you'll find all the other things (sand, smaller rocks, little frogs, etc…) will fit in fine.

Your days will get so much easier, and you'll procrastinate less. You'll get closer to your core goals and your sense of self-satisfaction will increase. Plus, you can reward yourself more often without feeling guilty. Not bad, eh?

There, you now have another way to plan your work and your days. Just remember how you spend the first few hours sets the mood for the rest of the day.

Now go and seize your day!

SO, HOW DO YOU FEEL?

That's the end of this section. Write down anything you didn't capture in the questions but that you want to get out of your system.

1. How do you feel after completing this section?

- ○ Meh. Nothing interesting here
- ○ I really want to get this, but I'm lost and need help
- ○ I'm doing well. Just need to think some more
- ○ Fantastic. I've nailed this round. Woo-hoo!
- ○ Other: _____

2. What do you still need to figure out?

A.

B.

C.

3. What three actions will you take in the next seven days to keep this topic on the top of your mind and clarify it further?

A.

B.

C.

SECTION FIVE MY PLEDGE

A promise to myself

No one changes the world who isn't obsessed.

Billie Jean King

MY PLEDGE

I pledge to take the time to create my annual goal map and execution plan.

I will stay focused on my goals and track the progress of my plans.

I will consider mistakes to be part of my journey. I will learn from them and move forward without looking back.

Today, I pledge to take action toward my future vision.

| **Signature** | |

| **Date** | |

Your Rebel Plans

SECTION SIX BONUS QUESTIONS

How well have I done this year?

Your Rebel Plans

Knowing what must be done does away with fear.

Rosa Parks

> *"All behavior is belief driven."*
> *Anonymous*

HAVE YOU DESTROYED YOUR LIMITATIONS?

Remember the first exercise you did in this book about your limitations?

Do you feel you're still holding on to those same limiting beliefs after going through all you have in this book? Or have you changed?

Go back to that exercise in the Introduction Section and ask yourself if you feel the same way, or if you've changed your mind. If you have shifted your mindset, write down your new beliefs—hopefully positive, progressive and unlimited ones!

1. The limitation I had:

How I feel about this limitation now:

My new unlimited belief:

2. The limitation I had:

How I feel about this limitation now:

My new unlimited belief:

Your Rebel Plans

3. The limitation I had:

How I feel about this limitation now:

My new unlimited belief:

4. The limitation I had:

How I feel about this limitation now:

My new unlimited belief:

5. The limitation I had:

How I feel about this limitation now:

My new unlimited belief:

"Self-awareness is probably the most important thing toward being a champion."
Billie Jean King

YEAR-END REFLECTIONS

You've come to the end of this workbook.

By now, you should have your goal map and execution plan—your treasure map to the future you desire. And you're now raring to start. But before I let you go, I want to share one more exercise to do at year-end.

Here's a list of questions that will help you take stock of your achievements and lessons learned at the end of every year. These ten questions are all about how you spent the past 365 days of your life. Come back on December 31st and see how you answer these questions.

Better yet, design your year ahead knowing you'll be asking yourself these questions twelve months later. Always begin with the end in mind, and you'll do well, my friend.

Good luck!

1. What were my biggest wins this year?

2. What were the biggest challenges I faced this year?

3. What did I love and truly enjoy doing this year?

4. Who were the most important people I hung out with or met this year?

5. What were the major new skills or knowledge areas I gained this year?

6. What were the biggest gains I made on my physical health front?

7. What were the biggest gains I made on my mental health front?

8. What have I outgrown (unnecessary things or unhealthy people) that I will leave behind as I move into a brand-new year?

9. What am I most grateful for that happened this year?

10. What were the biggest lessons I learned this year?

Your Rebel Plans

> *"You can waste your lives drawing lines. Or you can live your life crossing them."*
> Shonda Rhimes

FINAL WORD

Wow. I'm impressed. I commend you if you've stuck it out and come this far. Congratulations! You're a trooper.

You've accomplished visioning, goal setting, and planning. This is spectacular and will set you apart from 97 percent of people in the world who never set goals, or even if they do, have no idea how to get to them.

Remember, all these workbooks do is give you the tools to get you to your life's dreams. It's up to you to apply these ideas. Get out there and take action. Start today.

The third Rebel Diva book, *Your Rebel Life*, is a companion guide to the first two. It explores success habits hacks that will help you on your journey toward your vision. It introduces you to the ten most important pillars of your life and delves into each area to show how you can create a holistic, healthy and happy life. Isn't that what we all want?

See you in the next workbook!

Your Rebel Plans

"Just when the caterpillar thought the world was over, she became a butterfly."

English Proverb

Your Rebel Plans

THANK YOU!

Thank you for dedicating time for yourself and for coming on this journey to create an amazing, shiny new you. Keep this book somewhere you can see every day to keep the momentum going. Go over your answers regularly to check your progress and plan for the next year.

To continue your journey, get **Your Rebel Life**, the third Rebel Diva workbook today!

http://books2read.com/YourRebelLife

SIGN UP TO GET YOUR EXCLUSIVE GIFT!

This Rebel Diva booklet comes with three essential decision-making tools to help you overcome any anxieties when faced with life's challenges. Click on the cover or go to the link below to get your free copy and also learn about exclusive and free training at the Rebel Diva Academy.

THE FEAR BUSTER

https://www.rebeldivas.com/rebel-plans-gift/

Come on over and join other Rebel Divas in our
private **Facebook Group: Rebel Divas**
to share your thoughts and dreams, learn new tips and get inspired.

https://www.facebook.com/groups/RebelDivas

Your thoughts mean a lot to me and I'd love to hear your feedback. It's also how I'll be able to give you what you're looking for. If you'd like to leave an honest review of this book, please do so here:

http://books2read.com/YourRebelPlans

THE REBEL DIVA SERIES

www.RebelDivas.com

The Rebel Diva workbooks are practical guides to creating the life you dream about.

They share lessons from the best self-help and personal development resources available today and synthesize them into simple guided exercises that anyone can follow without drowning in detail.

These books don't just tell you what you need to do. They take you by the hand and show how to follow through.

The tools and techniques here are simple, but their reach is deep. They're designed to make you contemplate your past, present, and future, and make you a visionary for your own life.

All the answers are in you. All these workbooks do is extract them one gentle question at a time and make you write them down, so you can take the first step toward your future.

These books aren't for your bookshelf. They are to be marked up, highlighted, and dog-eared with your scribbling all over the pages. Keep them on your bedside table with a pen, so you can reach them whenever you need a jolt of inspiration or want to track your progress.

BOOK 1 - YOUR REBEL DREAMS

This book will show you how to discover your purpose and ultimate passions in life.

You'll find practical exercises to help you create a vision for your life that matches your personal values and your unique personality.

Once completed, check back with Your Rebel Dreams once a year. Make it the thing you do every December 31st, just before you head out to the New Year's Eve party.

Uncover the amazing gifts you have in life!

The main sections in this book are:

1. My Values
2. My Flair
3. My Zone
4. My Joy
5. My Service
6. My Vision

BOOK 2 - YOUR REBEL PLANS

This book will show you how to make your dreams come alive.

You'll go through a series of easy exercises to help you identify your core goals and create an action plan for your life.

You'll learn how to track your progress and celebrate your successes. At the end of this workbook, you'll have a treasure map to your life dreams—a map that will help you stay on your game, no matter what.

Once completed, check back with Your Rebel Plans every three months to see how you're progressing. And to find a good excuse to reward yourself! You only need to spend thirty minutes each time to make sure you're on track.

The main sections in this book are:

1. My Goals
2. My Plans
3. My Check-ins

4. My Schedule

5. My Year

BOOK 3 - YOUR REBEL LIFE

This book will show you how to live a harmonious, happy and healthy life every single day.

You'll get access to one hundred tips for the ten most important pillars of your life. You'll learn how to design an amazing lifestyle that's in tune with the fundamental values you identified in Your Rebel Dreams and the ambitions you wrote down in Your Rebel Plans.

This is a standalone guide and can be read anytime. Take a thirty-minute coffee break at the end of every month to take stock of where you are and apply one more tip to enhance your life.

The main sections in this book are:

Environment:
1. Feel Well - My Environment Health

Health:
2. Sleep Well - My Rejuvenation Health
3. Move Well - My Physical Health
4. Eat Well - My Nutrition Health

Vocation:
5. Learn Well - My Knowledge Health
6. Work Well - My Career Health
7. Invest Well - My Wealth Health

Spirit:
- 8. Think Well - My Mental Health
- 9. Love Well - My Relationship Health
- 10. Play Well - My Spirit Health

ABOUT THE AUTHOR

Tikiri holds a bachelor's degree in international business from North America and a master's degree in management from Europe. She has over fifteen years of experience managing large-scale projects and corporate risk management programs and has studied, worked and lived in several countries across four continents.

Tikiri is the award-winning author of several fiction and nonfiction books and through her writing, champions women's and girl's rights around the world.

Okay, enough of the formal stuff…

My expertise doesn't come from a postdoctoral psychology degree. Neither do I profess to be a self-help guru of any sort. I'm still a work in progress and try to learn something new every day.

I started small. Very small. I began my career trying to sell Kirby vacuum cleaners door-to-door (nope, I didn't sell even one) and graduated to cleaning toilets (made a lot more than my vacuum-selling stint). I did this to pay for rent, ramen noodles, and tuition.

Like everyone else, I've muddled my way through life. I've been a traveler and an immigrant. I've been poor and desperate. I've been bullied and afraid. I've been heartbroken and devastated. And I'm a foreigner everywhere I go. Through all this, I've also seized opportunities to learn as much as I can, push myself and figure out how people think, behave and grow.

The most important lesson I've learned is if you stand in your power no matter what's going around you or how others treat you, things work out. They always do.

I've used my personal experiences and what I've learned from others to write these books. The lessons in here are what helped me create the life I desired, so I wrote these books hoping they will help you too in some way. Even if one sentence spurs you forward, I will have done my job.

To say hello and connect, come on over to www.TikiriHerath.com

A FREE STORY

THE RED-HEELED REBELS NOVEL SERIES

This is a gripping, coming-of-age, global suspense thriller series with iron-willed heroines who fight villains and traditions that keep them down. If you like exotic locales, complex twists, and globe-trotting female leads, you'll love this story.

What readers are saying:

- "A wonderful story! I didn't want to leave the characters."
- "A real page-turner and international thriller. Reminds me of why I've always loved to read. Because I can visit worlds and places I wouldn't ordinarily get to see."
- "If you love adventure, strong female leads and cultural insights, this is the perfect book for you."
- "A heart-stopping adventure. I just couldn't put the book down till I finished reading it."
- "This is soul writing that needs to be read."

To claim the prequel story to this series for free, go to

www.RedHeeledRebels.com

Your Rebel Plans

Tikiri

Your Rebel Plans

www.ingramcontent.com/pod-product-compliance
Lightning Source LLC
Chambersburg PA
CBHW070052080526
44586CB00013B/1018